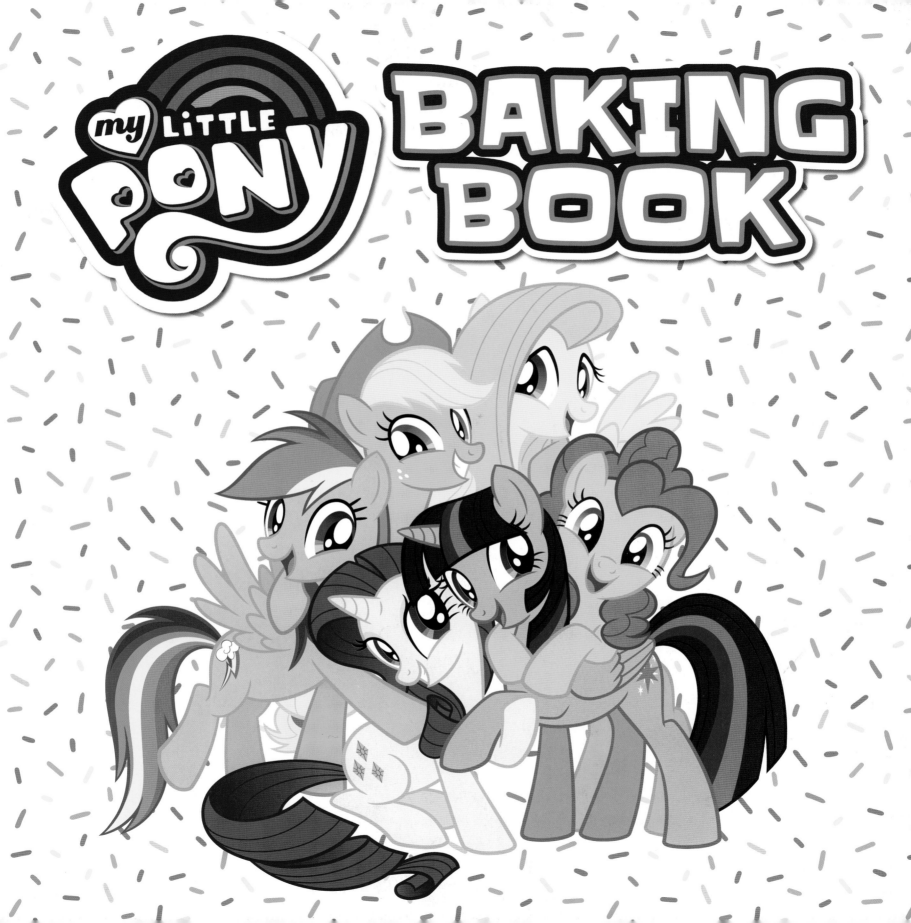

BAKING BOOK

Recipes and Photographs
by Christi Johnstone

MEDIA LAB BOOKS
NEW YORK

Table of Contents

Pointers for Parents

1. **Take your child shopping with you.**
   Buying the ingredients together can be a fun way to learn and to let your child help decide on flavors and colors. If allergies are a concern, older children can help read ingredients and call out anything that's not safe for them to eat.

2. **Bake with your child when you have plenty of time to do so—you don't want to feel rushed.**
   Also, read through each recipe before you decide to try it, as some require chilling the dough and will take longer to finish.

3. **Let your child help as much as they can with the baking.**
   Preschoolers can mix, pour in pre-measured ingredients, spread frosting and help decorate. For young children, you might want to break measurements down into smaller increments (for example, three ⅓ cups of flour instead of 1 cup of flour) to help draw out the activity and make the measuring cups easier for them to hold. You can challenge older children to read the recipes as well as measure ingredients.

4. **Go over kitchen safety with your child, including reading the safety tips on page 10.**
   Supervise your children closely if they are using knives or handling hot objects. Do not let your child eat uncooked dough or batter—you might choose to offer some "mix-ins" instead, like chocolate chips or other small candies.

5. **Accept that your kitchen is about to get messy, especially if your child is younger.**
   Just make sure they help you clean up afterward!

6. **Remember that no matter what your final results look like, they probably taste good!**
   Looks aren't everything, after all. Plus, baking together is a great way to help your child improve their science, math and reading skills. Delicious!

Pinkie Pie's Top 5½ Reasons for Baking

1. It's fun!

2. It's delicious!

3. You get to share the things you bake with your friends!

4. It's a great way to say, "I love you!"

5. Baked goods are the perfect present to bring to a party!

5½. Did I mention it's fun?

7 Baking Safety Rules for your Kids

Baking is the BEST, but it's a lot less fun when you burn your hoof or singe your mane. So you better make sure to follow these rules! I had Twilight Sparkle help me write them down, so you know they're legit.

Aw, thanks Pinkie Pie!

1. Kids Need to Ask First.

Let your kids know they need to ask permission to bake! Plus, depending on what you're baking, they might need your help with some of the trickier parts, like handling heavy equipment or taking things out of the oven.

2. Wash Your Hooves (err...Hands).

You're probably going to be touching dough or batter, and you don't want anything icky ending up in your food! Make sure your hands are clean when you start baking, and wash them again after handling dough, raw eggs or other ingredients.

3. Keep Your Space Clean.

Remember your ABCs: Always Be Cleaning! After you're done with an ingredient, put it away and make sure to throw out any trash you create, like butter wrappers or egg shells. An organized, clean space is safer and easier to work in. And, of course, if you drop something, clean the floor right away—you don't want anypony slipping and getting hurt!

4. Use a Potholder.

Always protect yourself from hot pans and cookie sheets with a potholder! Find a nice thick one that you can use comfortably.

5. Be Careful with Knives.
If you're chopping something like nuts or fruit for a recipe, show your child the proper way to hold and use a knife.

6. Don't Taste Raw Dough!
Even though it's very tempting to sneak a bite of cookie dough or lick some brownie batter, eating uncooked flour or eggs can make you sick. And nopony wants that!

7. Make Sure Kids Pay Attention and Listen.
It's extra important to always pay attention to what you're doing in the kitchen. You don't want them to burn the cookies (or themselves!) because they were careless or not listening. If everyone is smart, you'll all have fun and stay safe at the same time!

Reading a Recipe

Read the entire recipe at least once prior to beginning. Then take your time—most baking disasters happen because of rushing!

Check the Difficulty

The easiest recipes have the fewest steps and/or ingredients. And we didn't count decorations, because you can do those as simply as you like!

 = Easy

= Intermediate

= Advanced

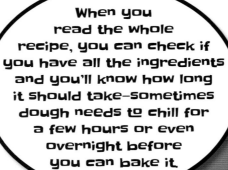

When you read the whole recipe, you can check if you have all the ingredients and you'll know how long it should take—sometimes dough needs to chill for a few hours or even overnight before you can bake it.

Did you know 3 teaspoons equals 1 tablespoon?

Common Abbreviations

Tbsp means tablespoon. Some other books might write it with just a capital "T."

tsp means teaspoon. Some other books might just use a lowercase "t."

cup is sometimes abbreviated as just "c."

Hint, pinch, smidgen, dash or tad are all different ways of saying, "Just a tiny bit!" You'll usually see this measurement for spices—it means the amount you can pinch between your fingers.

Substitutions

The recipes in this book have not been tested with any substitutions, and final results may differ—we recommend making them as written whenever possible!

Brown Sugar
1 cup light brown sugar = 1 cup white sugar + 1 Tbsp molasses

1 cup dark brown sugar = 1 cup white sugar + 2 Tbsp molasses

Butter
1 Tbsp butter = 1 Tbsp vegetable shortening (This is only recommended in small amounts. Do not use shortening to make frostings or glazes, or to replace the majority of butter in any recipe.)

Buttermilk
1 cup buttermilk = 1 Tbsp lemon juice or white vinegar + enough milk (any kind, even non-dairy!) to make 1 cup (add lemon juice to measuring cup and fill to 1 cup line with milk); let mixture stand for 5 minutes

1 cup buttermilk = 1 cup plain yogurt

Cake Flour
1 cup cake flour = 2 Tbsp cornstarch + $\frac{7}{8}$ cup sifted all-purpose flour (add cornstarch to measuring cup, then spoon in flour and level off)

Eggs
1 egg = 1 Tbsp ground flaxseed + 3 Tbsp water

Sour Cream
1 cup sour cream = 1 cup plain yogurt

Vegetable Oil
1 cup vegetable oil = 1 cup applesauce

Some of these are good to know if you need to make a recipe vegan!

A Baker Needs the Right Tools!

Sugarcube Corner has everything you could ever need to bake all kinds of stuff! Frosted cupcakes, rainbow cakes, birthday cakes, cute little cake pops, apple fritters, lemon cookies, cherry pies, fruit turnovers, berry oatmeal–

Uh, Pinkie Pie? I think we're all ready to look at those tools now.

Mixing Bowls
Everypony needs a set of these to mix up all their ingredients!

Measuring Spoons
These help you measure things you just need a little bit of, like baking soda, salt or vanilla extract.

Dry Measuring Cups
Use dry measuring cups for big amounts of dry ingredients, like flour and sugar. Choose dry measuring cups that can easily be leveled off with a flat edge, like a butter knife.

Liquid Measuring Cups
Liquid measuring cups are for anything liquid, like milk, honey or maple syrup.

Electric Mixer
Use this for creaming butter and sugar, whipping up cream and combining big batches of ingredients! But if you don't have one, you can still make just about anything—ponies were baking long before electric mixers were invented! Learn more about this in the techniques on p. 19.

Sifter or Fine Mesh Strainer
When measuring flour that's been sitting in a bag for a while, you might want to sift it first—it's probably more packed than you want it to be, and this gets rid of any clumps!

Whisk
Perfect for mixing together dry ingredients or making your own whipped cream by hand.

Wooden Spoons
Use these to mix together dough or batter by hand.

Rubber Spatula
You'll need one to get every last bit of batter out of your bowl.

Rolling Pin
There's no better tool for rolling out dough!

Silicone Baking Mat or Parchment Paper
Line your cookie sheets with these to keep your treats from sticking.

Cookie Sheets, Cake Pans and Muffin/ Cupcake Tins
Everything you need to bake and mold your tasty creations!

Cooling Rack
Help your baked goods get a little extra cool air once they're out of the oven.

Oven Mitts/Potholders
Don't touch a hot pan without one!

Measuring 101

Measuring Dry Ingredients

When measuring dry ingredients in measuring spoons or dry measuring cups, fill until it overflows and then level it off with the back of a knife. Try to do this over the ingredient container so you don't waste anything!

Extra Advice

Flour
When measuring flour, don't dig the measuring cup into the flour bag to scoop it out. Instead, use a spoon to heap it into the measuring cup and then level it off with a knife.

Brown sugar
When measuring brown sugar, pack it tightly into the measuring cup by pressing down with the back of a spoon, then level it off as usual.

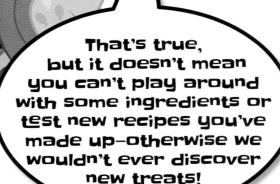

Baking is a precise science, so you need to be extra careful when you're measuring ingredients, right, Pinkie Pie?

That's true, but it doesn't mean you can't play around with some ingredients or test new recipes you've made up—otherwise we wouldn't ever discover new treats!

If you're measuring a sticky ingredient, like molasses or maple syrup, spray the inside of the measuring cup with nonstick cooking spray beforehand.

Then it should slide right out!

Peanut butter is sticky, but you should measure it as a dry ingredient!

Measuring Wet Ingredients

Measuring wet ingredients is usually pretty easy—just fill the liquid measuring cup to the right line! To make sure it's measured properly, set the cup on a level surface, like your counter, and crouch down so you're checking at eye level.

Ingredients are Important!

If you want your treats to come out delicious, you need to make sure everything you're using is delicious, too!

Check expiration dates!
If items like baking soda and baking powder are expired, baked goods won't rise properly.

Room temperature ingredients are the very best to bake with (unless a recipe explicitly tells you to use very cold ingredients, like cold butter for making pie crust). Whenever possible, and always when called for, let your ingredients sit at room temperature for a bit prior to starting your recipe.

Unless it calls for otherwise, all recipes use unsalted butter.
Speaking of butter, consistency matters! Some recipes call for melted butter, some call for cold and some call for softened. Softened butter shouldn't be melting, but you should be able to leave an indent in it with your finger.

Stick to the recipe, or use approved substitutions (see p. 13). Using margarine in place of butter won't give you the same results, and powdered sugar can't be substituted for granulated sugar.

There are a few ingredients you can pick and choose with, like sprinkles, food dyes and chocolate chips. Sprinkles and food dyes are simply for making things pretty and colorful, so you can skip them or swap them. While recipes in this book use semi-sweet chocolate chips, you can absolutely use milk chocolate or even dark chocolate chips. It will alter the taste slightly, but you'll still have great results. You can also switch up berries in many recipes, especially between raspberries, blackberries and blueberries.

I only use the very best carrots when making treats for Angel!

Time for the Oven!

Oven Tips and Tricks

1. Very few ovens are spot-on accurate temperature-wise, and many vary by 10–20 degrees. An inexpensive oven thermometer is a great way to make sure your recipes are baking at the correct temperature.

2. Give your preheated oven some time to sit! When an oven reaches temperature, it has only reached temperature in one part of the oven. Wait at least 10 minutes after reaching the desired temperature to make sure the temperature is even throughout. It's best to have your baking rack centered in your oven and only bake on one rack at a time.

3. Stay focused! It's always best to stay nearby when baking and keep an eye on your progress. Also, pay attention to your nose. Yes, your nose! Your nose is often the first thing to know something is ready to come out of the oven. If you start smelling something delicious, make sure to check its progress.

4. No peeking! OK, maybe a little (that's what the oven window is for!), but try to keep your oven door shut during baking. Every time the oven door opens, the temperature will drop—and that impacts your recipe.

5. The cook times in this book are based on baking in metal pans. If you are using glass pans, your recipes might bake faster. If using glass, start checking for doneness about 10 minutes earlier than the listed baking times.

Don't Forget to Prep Those Pans!

As a rule, always line your pans with parchment paper or foil: they're your baking BFFs.

Parchment paper is great for lining baking sheets when you make cookies, and you always want to line your cake pans with it in order to help get your cakes out of the pan after baking. Trace around your baking pan on a sheet of parchment paper, cut and then place it in the bottom of your pan. It might not be a perfect fit, but that's OK! Make sure to spray it and the sides with nonstick cooking spray or grease with butter.

Foil is perfect for lining an 8x8", 9x9" or 13x9" baking pan. Not only does it help prevent your items from sticking, but if you use enough foil so that some hangs over the edges, you can use those edges as handles to pull your baked goods out of the pan.

Finally, don't let things get sticky! Use either a nonstick cooking spray or generously grease and flour your pans as directed in recipes. Otherwise they might taste great but won't come out of the pan in one piece.

Terrific Techniques

Mixing

When using an electric mixer, it's important to always start on the low setting and to gently place the beaters in the ingredients before you turn it on. When mixing dry ingredients into wet ingredients, stir it a few times by hand before using the mixer—otherwise, you might send a lot of flour right out of the bowl!

It's also important to give your butter and sugar time to mix! Many recipes call for creaming butter and sugar for 2–3 minutes until light and fluffy. You'll see that the consistency changes and it really does get lighter and fluffier, but it does take time.

You can also bake without an electric mixer. It just requires a little extra time and a little upper-arm strength.

These are all the skills I use to make the most delicious treats at Sugarcube Corner!

To cream butter and sugar together without a mixer, start by mixing softened butter with a wooden spoon. Once the butter becomes light and fluffy, add the sugar and keep mixing until it's all incorporated. Occasionally, use a rubber spatula to get everything on the sides of the bowl mixed back in.

To whip cream without a mixer, first chill your bowl, whisk and cream in the refrigerator. Once everything's cold, just pour the cream in the bowl and whisk away until soft peaks form! Now is when you can add sugar to taste. Fold in the sugar, then continue whipping until you've reached the consistency you like. If you overdo it, add a little more cream and fold it in gently.

Testing for Doneness

Before you take a cake or muffin out to cool, test it for doneness by inserting a knife or toothpick in the center. If it comes out clean, it's done! If raw batter comes out on the knife, it needs a few more minutes.

I bet I could whip cream faster than any mixer in Ponyville!

Icing Tips

Make sure to let recipes cool properly.
If your brownies, cakes or bars are even the slightest bit warm, the frosting will start melting. As a rule of thumb, a cool or cold baked good is the easiest to frost, especially for cakes. Plus, trying to cut into a dessert prior to fully cooling it can be a messy endeavor!

To easily fill a piping bag with frosting,
open the bag and place it in a tall, heavy drinking glass. Fold the edges of the bag over the glass to help hold it open while you fill it.

When you're piping on icing,
slow and steady does the trick. Squeeze gently or you might have a frosting explosion!

Serving and Storing Tips

If you are cutting a cold dessert,
warming up a knife by running it under hot water (then drying it) will help. For cutting brownies, bars and even pies, a sturdy disposable plastic knife is perfect. Plastic knives are naturally nonstick and they can give you a very clean cut.

Want to keep your baked goods—especially cookies—soft?
Add a piece of simple sandwich bread to the container you are storing them in. When the bread dries out, replace it. It's like the bread casts a magic spell on your treats and keeps them from drying out too quickly!

Extra Advice

If you're piping on icing, you might need to make a little extra because some of it will get stuck on the inside of the piping bag. Also, if you don't have a piping bag, you can use a plastic sandwich bag—just cut the tip off one corner.

For professional-looking cupcakes without using an icing bag, use your finger to gently swirl the icing, starting on the outside and making concentric circles toward the center. Or use everypony's favorite decoration: sprinkles!

How to Frost a Layer Cake

Each layer of the cake should be a similar height with a flat top in order to stack cake.
If cake has a domed top, have an adult help level the cake using a serrated knife to skim off the domed part of the cake.

Cakes are easiest to frost when they are cold.
Placing cake layers in a refrigerator or freezer ahead of time and allowing them to chill, or even partially freeze, will make frosting the cake easier.

Place the first layer of the cake on a cake plate or cake stand.
To keep the cake plate clean, set the cake on torn pieces of parchment paper or foil that you can gently pull out once you are done frosting. (Directions continue at top of next page.)

First,

spoon approximately ½–1 cup of frosting onto the top of the cake layer, and use a small offset spatula to smooth frosting into an even layer covering the top of the layer. Place the next layer on the cake and repeat the process until all layers are on the cake. If some frosting comes out the sides, this is fine.

Next,

use approximately 1 cup of frosting to cover the cake with a "crumb coat," or a very light layer of frosting. A crumb coat will help seal any of the crumbs into the cake. It's OK if this is messy; another layer of frosting will cover it. Once a light coat of frosting covers the entire cake, place cake in refrigerator to chill for at least 20 minutes.

After chilling cake,

the final (colored, if you like) layer of frosting can be added to the cake. Frosting can be smoothed on with an offset spatula or piped on using a piping bag and piping tips.

These directions are extra helpful for the Purple Velvet Cake (p. 104) and Magic Mix Cake (p. 106)!

Best Buttercream Frosting

This recipe makes enough to frost a three-layer cake.
Use half the recipe for smaller batches of cupcakes or single-layer cakes.

2   cups butter, softened
8–10 cups powdered sugar, sifted to
        remove any lumps
3   tsp vanilla extract
¼   tsp salt
4   Tbsp room-temperature heavy
        cream or half-and-half, plus
        more if needed
        Food coloring

1. With an electric mixer, cream butter until light and fluffy, about 3–5 minutes. Butter should become a very pale yellow color.

2. Add powdered sugar, 1 cup at a time. After each cup, mix well until powdered sugar is fully incorporated. Continue until you have added 8 cups of powdered sugar.

3. Add vanilla, salt and heavy cream, and mix until well-combined. If a firmer frosting is desired, add more powdered sugar (¼ cup at a time). Add more heavy cream (1 tsp at a time) if a thinner frosting is preferred.

4. (Opt) If frosting a three-layer cake, set aside about 4 cups of frosting for the filling and

crumb coat. To color remaining frosting a single color, simply add food coloring directly to the remaining frosting bowl and mix well until combined. wAdd additional food coloring until desired shade is reached. For multiple colors of frosting, divide frosting into multiple bowls, then color each bowl independently.

For a truly white frosting, use a clear imitation vanilla extract. Other vanilla extracts will create a slightly yellow frosting.

These are the best cookie recipes anypony has ever seen— I guarantee it!

Cookies

Whip up a batch or two for your next party, sleepover or Saturday night!

Chocolate Chip
Cookies, p.34

Peanut Butter Candy Cookies

Makes 3 dozen cookies

What pony doesn't love peanut butter?

Ingredients

1½ cups creamy peanut butter
1 cup butter, softened
1 cup light brown sugar
1 cup granulated sugar
2 eggs
1 tsp vanilla extract
2 cups all-purpose flour

1½ tsp baking soda
½ tsp salt
1–2 cups Reese's Pieces® candies
½ cup chocolate chips
½ cup peanut butter chips
½ cup mini peanut butter cups, coarsely chopped

Directions

1. Preheat oven to 350°F.

2. With a mixer, beat together peanut butter, butter and sugars until creamy and well combined. Add in eggs and vanilla and beat until creamy.

3. Add flour, baking soda and salt to mixture and mix until just combined. Fold in Reese's Pieces®, chocolate chips, peanut butter chips and chopped mini peanut butter cups.

4. Scoop cookies onto a cookie sheet that has been lined with a silicone mat. Each scoop should hold about 2 Tbsp of dough.

5. Bake for 12–14 minutes. Remove from oven and allow cookies to cool on baking sheet for at least 10 minutes, then transfer to wire rack to continue cooling.

Freeze peanut butter cups for a few hours prior to using. This will help keep them from completely melting in the oven.

Hey Big Mac, can you help me make a batch of these cookies?

Eeyup!

Soft Sugar Cookies

Makes 2 dozen cookies

Make this fun frosting in any color you like!

Ingredients

Cookies
1	cup granulated sugar
12	Tbsp butter, softened
2	eggs
½	cup full-fat sour cream
1	tsp vanilla extract
3¼	cups all-purpose flour
1½	tsp baking powder
½	tsp baking soda
½	tsp salt

Frosting
12	Tbsp butter, softened
2½	cups powdered sugar
1	tsp vanilla extract
1–2	Tbsp milk or cream
	Food coloring
	Sprinkles for decorating

Directions

1. Cream the sugar and butter together with an electric mixer until light and fluffy, about 2–3 minutes.

2. Add the eggs, sour cream and vanilla to butter and mix well to combine.

3. In a separate bowl, mix flour, baking powder, baking soda and salt. Add the dry ingredients to the wet ingredients and mix well.

4. Transfer dough to an airtight container and place in refrigerator for at least one hour. Note that this dough will be soft and sticky.

5. When ready to bake, preheat the oven to 350°F. Line two baking sheets with parchment paper or silicone baking mats.

6. Remove cookie dough from refrigerator and use a cookie scoop to scoop a ball of dough that is about the size of a golf ball into your hands and shape into a smooth ball. If dough is still sticky, dust your hands with flour. Once shaped, place the balls of dough onto cookie sheets at least 2 inches apart. Gently press down and slightly flatten each ball of dough with your hands.

7. Bake the cookies 10–12 minutes, until they puff up and are starting to just slightly brown around edges. Place the baking sheet on a wire cooling rack. Allow cookies to cool on baking sheet for at least 10 minutes.

8. To make frosting, cream the butter and powdered sugar with an electric mixer until light and fluffy, about 2–3 minutes. Add in vanilla and mix well. If the frosting is stiff, beat in the milk or cream one tablespoon at a time until desired consistency is reached. Add food coloring and mix well until desired color is obtained.

9. Pipe frosting onto cookies with a piping bag, or use an offset spatula to frost cookies. Top with sprinkles after frosting.

Notes This frosting does not truly firm up, so it's best not to stack cookies on top of each other.

Pile on the sprinkles and these cookies are absolutely perfect!

S'mores Cookies

Makes 3 dozen cookies

All the flavors you love, even without a campfire!

Ingredients

1	cup cold butter, cubed
1¼	cups sugar
2	large eggs
½	cup dark or regular cocoa powder
2¼	cups all-purpose flour
¼	tsp salt
1	tsp baking powder
1	cup chocolate chips
1	cup dehydrated marshmallows, such as Kraft Mallow Bits®
1	cup broken graham crackers, about the size of chocolate chips

Directions

1. Preheat oven to 350°F.

2. In the bowl of an electric mixer, combine the butter and sugar. Beat together on medium-high speed until light and fluffy, about 2–3 minutes.

3. Blend in the eggs one at a time, scraping down the bowl as needed. Add in the cocoa powder and mix until well blended.

4. Add the flour, salt and baking powder to the bowl and mix on low speed just until incorporated. Fold in the chocolate chips, dehydrated marshmallows and crushed graham crackers.

5. Stir to combine or, if needed, transfer the dough to a work surface and knead briefly by hand to be sure the ingredients are well combined. This dough is very thick.

6. Using standard size cookie scoops, scoop 1 ½ Tbsp dough onto cookie sheets 2 inches apart.

7. Bake for about 10 minutes. Let cool for 10 minutes on cookie sheets, then transfer to a wire rack to cool completely.

This works best with dehydrated mini-marshmallows, like the ones in hot cocoa. Kraft Mallow Bits are available in grocery stores, either in the baking section or the coffee and cocoa section. Regular ones can be used, but they can be extremely sticky once baked.

Let's take these on our next camping trip!

Birthday Cookie Cake

Makes 8 servings

This birthday treat is perfect for anypony who can't get enough cookies!

Ingredients

Cookie Cake
10	Tbsp butter, softened
⅔	cup light brown sugar
⅓	cup granulated sugar
1	whole egg, plus 1 egg yolk
1	tsp vanilla extract
1⅔	cups all-purpose flour
¾	tsp baking soda
¾	tsp salt
1	cup chocolate chips

Frosting
4	Tbsp butter, softened
2	Tbsp cocoa powder
1¼	cups powdered sugar
¼	tsp salt
½	tsp vanilla extract
1–2	Tbsp milk
	Food coloring
	Sprinkles for garnish

Directions

1. Preheat oven to 350°F.

2. Cut a circle of parchment paper into a circle to cover the bottom of a 9" or 10" cake pan. Place in pan and spray paper and sides with nonstick cooking spray.

3. Cream together butter and sugars with an electric mixer until light and fluffy, about 2 minutes.

4. Add egg, egg yolk and vanilla to mixture and mix well to combine.

5. Add flour, baking soda and salt to mixture and mix until just combined.

6. Fold in chocolate chips.

7. Spoon cookie dough into prepared pan and smooth with the back of a spoon to create a uniform layer.

8. Bake for 21–23 minutes.

9. Remove from oven and allow to cool completely.

10. Once cool, carefully run a knife around the edges of the cookie in the pan to help loosen it from the sides. Carefully invert to remove from the pan and place on a plate. Make sure to check if parchment paper is stuck on the bottom of the cookie cake, and if so peel to remove.

11. To make frosting, combine butter, cocoa, powdered sugar and salt in a mixing bowl and beat with an electric mixer until smooth. Add in vanilla and stir to combine.

12. Add 1 tablespoon of milk and beat with mixer to combine well. If a thinner texture is desired, add an additional tablespoon of milk. More milk can be added, one teaspoon at a time, to thin out consistency further, if desired.

13. Transfer frosting to a piping bag fitted with a large open star tip and pipe frosting around edges of cookie cake. Garnish with sprinkles.

A cookie instead of a cake? Now that's a trendy twist!

A 9" or 10" springform pan is ideal for this recipe, but a non-springform pan will work too—just make sure to place a parchment paper circle in the bottom of the pan and spray generously with nonstick cooking spray.

Brown Sugar Snickerdoodles

Makes 3 dozen cookies

Simple and delicious snickerdoodles are a top pony pick!

Sharing some of these could start a new friendship!

Ingredients

Cookies
4 cups flour
1 tsp baking soda
½ tsp baking powder
2 eggs
1 tsp cream of tartar
1 tsp cinnamon
1 cup butter

¾ cup granulated sugar
1 cup firmly packed light brown sugar
¼ cup milk
1 tsp vanilla

Toppings
6 Tbsp sugar
1 tsp cinnamon

Directions

1. In a bowl, sift together the flour, baking soda, baking powder, cream of tartar and cinnamon. Set aside.

2. In a separate bowl, cream the butter and sugars until fluffy. Add the eggs, milk and vanilla. Mix well.

3. Stir in the dry ingredients. Stir until just combined.

4. Cover bowl (or remove dough from bowl and wrap in plastic wrap) and chill for at least 2 hours, but not more than 24 hours.

5. When ready to bake, preheat oven to 350°F.

6. Form the dough into 1-inch balls. Mix cinnamon and sugar in a small bowl and roll each ball of dough through the cinnamon and sugar mixture to coat well.

7. Place on a greased baking sheet or a cookie sheet covered with wax paper or silicone baking mat.

8. Bake 8–9 minutes. Do not overbake. Allow to cool on baking sheet for at least 10 minutes before transferring to a wire cooling rack.

33

Make sure melted butter is not too hot prior to beginning this recipe to prevent sugars from melting and eggs from cooking!

Chocolate Chip Cookies

Makes 36 cookies

Add a little color to this classic with lots of sprinkles!

You can use any kind of chocolate chips or small candies!

Ingredients

1	cup unsalted butter, melted and cooled for 5–10 minutes	3	cups all-purpose flour
1	cup granulated sugar	2	tsp cornstarch
1	cup packed light brown sugar	1	tsp baking powder
2	eggs	1	tsp baking soda
1	tsp vanilla extract	1	tsp salt
¼	cup pure maple syrup	1½	cups semi-sweet chocolate chips
		½	cup assorted sprinkles

Directions

1. In a large bowl, combine melted butter and sugars. Stir well to combine.

2. Add eggs one at a time, stirring well after each addition.

3. Add in vanilla extract and maple syrup and stir well to combine.

4. In a separate bowl, combine flour, cornstarch, baking powder, baking soda and salt. Stir to combine.

5. Add flour mixture to wet ingredients and stir until combined.

6. Fold in chocolate chips and sprinkles and stir until combined.

7. Allow cookie dough to chill in refrigerator for at least 1 hour, but no more than 24 hours.

8. When ready to bake, preheat oven to 350°F.

9. Using a 2–3 tablespoon-sized cookie scoop, scoop dough onto cookie sheet, leaving 2 inches of space around each cookie to allow for spreading.

10. Bake 13–15 minutes, or until edges start to turn golden brown.

11. Remove from oven and allow to cool on cookie sheet for at least 10 minutes, then transfer cookies to a wire rack to finish cooling.

12. Repeat with remaining dough until all cookies are baked.

Optional
Add additional sprinkles to the tops of cookie dough scoops just prior to baking.

Fruity Fun Cookies

Makes 24 cookies

Everypony loves a sweet, fruity treat!

Ingredients

2	cups flour
¼	tsp salt
¾	cup butter, softened
	Yellow food coloring
1	cup granulated sugar
1	egg
1	Tbsp finely grated lemon peel
1	tsp lemon extract
½	cup sanding sugar or coarse sugar

Directions

1. Mix flour and salt in medium bowl. Set aside.

2. Beat butter and granulated sugar in large bowl with electric mixer on medium speed until light and fluffy. Add egg, lemon peel, extract and food coloring. Mix well.

3. Gradually beat in flour mixture on low speed until well mixed.

4. Divide dough in half. Form each half into a log about 9" long and 1½" in diameter. Wrap in wax paper. Refrigerate 1 hour or until firm. Preheat oven to 350°F.

5. Pour sanding sugar on large plate or wax paper. Roll each cold dough log in mixture to sugar-coat the outside evenly.

6. Cut dough into ¼" thick slices. Place on ungreased baking sheets.

7. Bake 12–15 minutes, or until lightly browned around edges.

8. Cool on baking sheets for at least 10 minutes prior to moving to wire racks to cool completely.

Notes This recipe makes lemon cookies, but you can make lime cookies with green food coloring, lime peel and lemon extract; orange cookies with orange food coloring, orange peel and orange extract; or raspberry cookies with pink food coloring, lemon peel and raspberry extract.

These cookies are the best part of a pony tea party!

Sanding sugar or coarse sugar can usually be found wherever you buy your sprinkles. You can buy it colored or color your own by combining sugar and a drop of food coloring in a zipper-style plastic bag and shaking very well to combine. Pour it out onto a large plate or sheet of wax paper to allow it time to dry.

Get creative with your mix-ins! Try chocolate chips, peanut butter chips, white chocolate chips, raisins, nuts...almost anything can be used in a Chaos Cookie.

Chaos Cookies

I think these are rather charming!

Makes 3 dozen cookies

These treats are a mix of everypony's favorite things!

Ingredients

1 cup butter, softened	½ tsp salt
1 cup granulated sugar	3 cups old-fashioned or quick-cooking
1 cup brown sugar	oats (not instant oats)
2 large eggs	½ cup chocolate chips
2 tsp vanilla	½ cup peanut butter or butterscotch
2 cups all-purpose flour	chips
1 tsp baking soda	1 cup M&M's® candies
1 tsp baking powder	

Directions

1. In a mixing bowl or stand mixer, beat butter and sugars together until light and creamy, about 2–3 minutes.

2. Mix in eggs, one at a time, until well combined, but do not overmix. Mix in vanilla.

3. In a large bowl, mix flour, baking soda, baking powder and salt.

4. Pour flour mixture into butter and sugar mixture and stir to combine well.

5. Add in oats, chocolate chips, peanut butter/butterscotch chips and M&M's® candies. Stir until well combined, but do not overmix.

6. Place cookie dough in a sealed container and put in refrigerator to chill for at least 30 minutes, but no more than 24 hours. Once ready to bake, preheat oven to 350°F.

7. Scoop cookie dough, about 2 tablespoons at a time, and place 2 inches apart on a cookie sheet that has been lined with a silicone baking mat or sprayed lightly with nonstick cooking spray.

8. Bake for 11–13 minutes, or until starting to turn golden brown.

9. Let cool on baking sheet for about 10 minutes, then transfer to a wire rack for cooling. Repeat process with remaining cookie dough.

Notes Chilling the dough helps to create a nice, thick, chewy cookie. This step can be skipped, but cookies will spread a bit more than if the dough was chilled.

Apple Cider Snaps

Makes 2 dozen cookies

Whip up a batch after a day in the orchard!

Ingredients

Cookies

¾	cup unsalted butter, softened
1	cup granulated sugar
1	large egg
¼	cup molasses
2½	cups all-purpose flour
2	tsp baking soda
½	tsp salt
½	tsp cinnamon
½	tsp ginger

Glaze

2	cups powdered sugar
½	tsp vanilla extract
3	Tbsp apple cider

Directions

1. Preheat oven to 350°F.

2. Mix together butter and sugar until light and fluffy, about 2–3 minutes, with an electric mixer.

3. Add egg and molasses and mix well.

4. In a separate bowl, combine flour, baking soda, salt, cinnamon and ginger, stirring to combine.

5. Add dry ingredients to wet ingredients and mix until well combined.

6. Form or scoop balls of dough that are slightly smaller than a golf ball.

Place them on a baking sheet 2–3 inches apart to allow room for cookies to spread.

7. Bake for 10–12 minutes. Remove from oven and allow cookies to cool on baking sheet for about 10 minutes, then transfer to a wire rack to finish cooling.

8. To make glaze, combine powdered sugar, vanilla and apple cider, stirring well to combine. If glaze is thicker than preferred, add ½ teaspoon more apple cider, then mix well. Repeat until desired consistency is reached.

9. Place a spoonful of glaze on the top of each cookie. Glaze will remain slightly tacky so avoid stacking cookies for 4–6 hours.

Y'all need to make these snappy snacks right away!

Out-of-
this-World
Brownies, p. 56

Brownies & Bars

They may have four corners, but these baked goods are anything but square!

These sweet treats are perfect for sharing with anypony!

Giddy-Up Granola Bars

Makes 12 bars

Take a time "oat" and snack on these yummy bars!

Ingredients

2½	cups rolled oats (not quick-cook oats)
⅓	cup honey
¼	cup butter
¼	cup brown sugar
1	tsp vanilla extract
¼	tsp salt
½	cup mini chocolate chips
1	Tbsp rainbow sprinkles

Directions

1. Preheat oven to 350°F.

2. Spread oats onto a large cookie sheet and place in the oven for 8 minutes to lightly toast. Remove from oven and allow to cool. Turn off oven; no further baking is required.

3. In a heavy saucepan, combine honey, butter and brown sugar. Stir over medium heat until butter melts, sugar dissolves and the mixture is combined. Remove from heat, add in vanilla and salt, and allow to cool at least 10 minutes.

4. Once both the oats and liquid mixtures have cooled slightly, place both in a bowl and stir well to combine. Once combined, stir in mini chocolate chips.

5. Spoon mixture into an 8x8" or 9x9" pan that has been lined with nonstick foil or parchment paper, and sprayed lightly with nonstick cooking spray. Once mixture is in the pan, sprinkle assorted sprinkles on top, then pat and press the mixture down firmly into pan.

6. Place pan in refrigerator and chill for at least 4 hours. Finally, remove from pan and cut into 12 bars.

It's very important to really press the mixture into the pan for 1–2 minutes. This step is what will help your granola stay in bar form.

I always keep these handy for late-night study sessions!

It works well to store these bars in the refrigerator, individually wrapped in foil. Take them out as needed, with a few minutes to come to room temperature prior to serving.

Candy Bar Brownies

Makes 16 brownies

Even if you don't add candy bars, this recipe still makes amazing brownies!

I just love peanut butter and chocolate!

Ingredients

Brownies
½   cup butter
1   cup sugar
1   tsp vanilla extract
2   eggs, room temperature
⅓   cup natural cocoa powder
     (not Dutch process)
½   cup flour
¼   tsp salt
¼   tsp baking powder
1   cup mini peanut butter
     cups, coarsely chopped

Frosting
⅓   cup butter
⅓   cup milk
1¼   cups sugar
1   tsp vanilla
1   cup semi-sweet
     chocolate chips

Toppings
Assorted candy bars and candy
of your choice, chopped
into bite-sized pieces

Fun-size candy bars are perfect for this recipe!

Directions

1. Preheat oven to 350°F. Line an 8x8" baking pan with foil and spray with nonstick cooking spray.

2. In a large, microwavable bowl, heat butter for 30 seconds, remove and stir. Repeat if more time is needed to melt butter. Allow melted butter to cool about 5 minutes.

3. Add sugar and vanilla to melted butter and stir well to combine.

   Add eggs and stir to combine. Add cocoa, flour, salt and baking powder, and stir to combine. Fold in chopped peanut butter cups. Spoon batter into prepared pan and spread into an even layer.

4. Bake 35–30 minutes, remove from oven and allow to cool.

5. To make frosting, combine butter, milk and sugar in a small

   saucepan and bring to a boil over medium-high heat.

6. Boil 45–60 seconds, then remove from heat.

7. Add in vanilla and chocolate chips and stir well until smooth. Pour over brownies, then garnish with candy. Allow 2–3 hours for frosting to set before serving.

Rainbow Magic Cookie Bars

Makes 16 bars

Rainbow Dash's favorite bars are bursting with color!

Ingredients

½	cup butter, melted
1½	cups graham cracker crumbs
1	(14-oz) can sweetened condensed milk
1	cup chocolate chips
1	cup milk chocolate M&M's® candies
1⅓	cups flaked coconut

I like to top these bars with even more rainbow sprinkles!

Directions

1. Preheat oven to 350°F (325°F for glass dish). Coat 13x9" baking pan with nonstick cooking spray.

2. Combine butter and graham cracker crumbs. Press into bottom of prepared pan.

3. Pour sweetened condensed milk evenly over crumb mixture. Layer evenly with chocolate chips, M&M's® candies and coconut. Press down firmly with a fork.

4. Bake 25 minutes, or until lightly browned. Allow to cool completely prior to serving.

You can try different colors or varieties of M&M's® candies in your Rainbow Magic Cookie Bars.

Frosted Sugar Cookie Bars

Makes 16 servings

Make these bars with any colors you like!

I love giving these as party favors!

Ingredients

Bars

½	cup butter, softened
1	cup granulated sugar
1	large egg
2	Tbsp sour cream
2	tsp pure vanilla extract
2⅓	cups all purpose flour

½	tsp baking powder
½	tsp salt

Frosting

½	cup butter, softened
2	cups powdered sugar
1–2	Tbsp milk
1	tsp vanilla extract
	Food coloring (opt)
	Sprinkles to decorate

Directions

1. Preheat oven to 375°F.

2. Line a 9x13" baking pan with foil and spray with nonstick cooking spray.

3. Combine butter and sugar in a bowl and mix with electric mixer until light and fluffy, about 2–3 minutes.

4. Add egg, sour cream and vanilla to mixture and beat until combined.

5. Add flour, baking powder and salt to mixture and stir until just combined. Do not overmix.

6. Scoop dough into baking pan and use fingers to distribute dough evenly over bottom of pan.

7. Bake for about 15 minutes or until the center appears set and sides are starting to lightly brown. Do not overbake. Remove from oven and allow to cool prior to frosting.

8. To make frosting, combine butter and powdered sugar in a bowl and mix with electric mixer until well-combined. Add milk and vanilla and mix until well combined. If a thinner frosting is desired, add more milk, one teaspoon at a time. If desired, add food coloring to frosting.

9. Spread frosting over bars. Top with sprinkles.

Make sure not to overbake, as these bars keep baking even after removed from the oven.

Apple Cheesecake Crumb Bars

Makes 16 bars

These bars are extra good with Granny Smith apples!

I like mine topped with a drizzle of caramel!

Ingredients

Apple Cheesecake Layer
- 2 cups all-purpose flour
- ½ cup firmly packed brown sugar
- ¾ cup cold butter, cut into cubes
- 2 (8-oz) bricks cream cheese, softened
- ½ cup, plus 2 Tbsp sugar, divided
- 1 tsp vanilla extract
- 2 large eggs
- 3 medium apples, chopped into ¼–½" pieces
- 1 tsp ground cinnamon
- ¼ tsp ground nutmeg

Crumb Topping
- ¾ cup flour
- ¾ cup firmly packed brown sugar
- ½ cup quick-cook oats
- ⅓ cup cold butter, cut into cubes

Directions

1. Preheat oven to 350°F.

2. In a food processor, combine and pulse flour, brown sugar and cold butter cubes until a crumb-type mixture forms. Press into a 13x9" pan that has been lined with either parchment paper or foil and sprayed lightly with nonstick cooking spray. Bake for 15 minutes and remove from oven.

3. Using an electric mixer, beat cream cheese until light and fluffy. Add ½ cup sugar and vanilla and beat until smooth. Add eggs, one at a time, and mix until just combined. Spread mixture over crust. Be careful as pan will be hot from the oven.

4. In a bowl, combine chopped apples, cinnamon, nutmeg and remaining 2 tablespoons of sugar. Stir to combine. Sprinkle apple mixture over cream cheese mixture.

5. In your food processor, combine flour, brown sugar, oats and remaining cold cubed butter. Pulse until mixture starts to form crumbs. Sprinkle this topping over the apples.

6. Bake for 25–30 minutes or until filling is set. Remove from oven. Once cooled to room temperature, transfer to refrigerator. Store in refrigerator.

Make sure the brownies are completely cool prior to assembling. You can even place them in the refrigerator before assembling to help chill them.

Brownie Ice Cream Sandwiches

Makes 16 servings

Make these when you want to bake something for a hot summer day!

Ingredients

1	pkg family-sized (13x9" pan) brownie mix, as well as listed ingredients
1½	quarts ice cream in flavor of your choice
	Sprinkles to garnish (opt)

Directions

1. Preheat oven to 350°F.

2. Line two 9x9" baking pans with foil, allowing the foil to hang over the edges of each pan by 3–4" to create a handle later. Spray foil-lined pans with nonstick cooking spray.

3. Prepare brownie mix according to package directions. Divide batter and spread half into the bottom of each prepared pan.

4. Bake 20–23 minutes, or until brownies are set in the center. Remove from oven and allow to cool in pan completely prior to assembling ice cream sandwiches.

5. When ready to assemble, let ice cream thaw at room temperature to soften, about 10 minutes. Once softened, scoop ice cream onto one pan of brownies and quickly smooth it out with a spatula or back of a spoon. Carefully remove the brownies from the other pan in one piece and place on top of ice cream. Place a piece of wax or parchment paper over top of brownies.

6. If pans are identical in size, place the bottom of the empty pan onto the top of the ice cream sandwich and press down to help weigh it down. Otherwise, press down firmly and evenly with your hands to help compress the ice cream sandwich.

7. Place in freezer for at least 4 hours to allow ice cream to firm up. When ready to serve, remove from freezer and gently run a warm knife around the edges of the pan to loosen. Use handles created by foil to lift out of pan.

8. Place on cutting board and cut into squares. If desired, the sides of ice cream sandwiches can be dipped in sprinkles for garnish.

Running a knife under hot water is a great way to warm it for cutting.

Mmmm— ice cream sandwiches are my favorite!

Out-of-this-World Brownies

Makes 16 brownies

They're the best in the ponyverse!

Ingredients

Brownies

10	Tbsp butter, melted
1¼	cups granulated sugar
¾	cup, plus 2 Tbsp unsweetened cocoa powder
½	tsp salt
2	large eggs
1	tsp pure vanilla extract
½	cup all-purpose flour
1	tsp baking powder
½	cup chocolate chips (opt)

Ganache Frosting

4	oz semi-sweet chocolate, chopped
4	oz milk chocolate, chopped
½	cup heavy cream
1	Tbsp room temperature butter, cut into small pieces
	Sprinkles for garnish

Directions

1. Preheat oven to 325°F. Line an 8" square pan with parchment paper or aluminum foil. Spray with nonstick cooking spray.

2. Combine melted butter, sugar, cocoa powder and salt in a large bowl and mix very well by hand for at least 2 minutes. If melted butter was hot, allow mixture to cool for 5–10 minutes before next step.

3. Add eggs, one at a time, mixing very well after each egg. Add in vanilla and mix.

4. Add flour and baking powder and mix very well, stirring for about 40 strokes. Fold in chocolate chips.

5. Bake 20–25 minutes, until a tester comes out with some moist crumbs attached. Do not overbake. Allow to cool on a wire rack.

6. To make ganache frosting, place chocolate in a heat-safe bowl. Warm heavy cream in a small saucepan on the stove until it just starts to bubble.

7. Pour hot cream over chocolate in bowl and let sit for about 30 seconds, then gently and consistently stir until all chocolate melts. Once chocolate has melted, add in butter and stir until well combined.

8. Pour chocolate ganache over the top of the chocolate brownies while the brownies are still warm. Brownies need to sit 3–4 hours for ganache to firm up prior to cutting. Add sprinkles before cooling.

I love making these brownies during study breaks!

There's nothing quite as scrumptious as homemade pie!

Pies, Crisps & Cobblers

If you like a crisp crust and a sweet filling, this section is for you!

Chocolate
Dream Pie, p. 72

Chimi-Cherry-Changa

Makes 6 servings

Or a chimi-cherry, or a cherry-changa—which sounds funniest?

This recipe can also be made with blueberry, strawberry or raspberry pie filling!

Ingredients

6	(8") soft flour tortillas
8	oz cream cheese, softened
4	tsp sugar
1	tsp vanilla extract
1½	cups cherries from cherry pie filling
2	Tbsp butter, melted
⅔	cup sugar
1½	tsp cinnamon

Directions

1. Preheat oven to 400°F.

2. In a bowl, combine cream cheese, sugar and vanilla. Mix well until smooth and combined.

3. Place a spoonful of cream cheese mixture onto the center of each tortilla and spread, leaving the outer inch of the tortilla free of the mixture.

4. Add about ¼ cup of cherries onto the top of the cream cheese on each tortilla.

5. Fold sides and one end over filling and roll up each tortilla. Secure with a toothpick or simply place seam side down on a baking pan.

6. Combine remaining ⅔ cup sugar and cinnamon in a bowl and stir to combine.

7. Brush the top and sides of each chimi-cherry-changa with melted butter and roll in cinnamon sugar mixture to coat, then return to baking sheet.

8. Bake 8–10 minutes, or until they start to brown.

9. Remove from oven and allow to cool prior to serving—the cherry mixture can stay quite hot!

I made these up myself!

Sprinkle Tarts

Makes 10 Tarts

Make these in any shape you'd like!

Ingredients

Tarts
2 rolls store-bought pie crust
⅓ cup (approximately) jam of your choice

Glaze
1 cup powdered sugar, sifted
2 Tbsp half-and-half or whole milk
Food coloring of your choice
Sprinkles of your choice

Directions

1. Preheat oven to 400°F.

2. Unroll the first pie crust onto a silicone mat or a work surface that has been lightly sprinkled with flour. Using a rolling pin, lightly roll out the pie crust to uniformly flatten. Do not roll too much or pie crust will be too thin.

3. Using a 3–4-inch cookie cutter, cut out as many shapes as possible and transfer to a baking sheet that has been lined with parchment paper or a silicone baking mat.

4. Add a spoonful of jam to the center of half your shaped pieces of pie crust. The amount will vary based on the size of your shapes. Make sure to keep the jam in the center, and allow room around it to seal your tart shut.

5. Place the remaining pie crust pieces on top of the jam covered pieces. Gently press and pinch the dough shut around the edges on each piece, then crimp the edges with the end of a fork all the way around. Using the fork, pierce the top of each one 2–3 times to allow steam to be released while baking. Place tray in refrigerator for 15 minutes and repeat process with remaining ingredients.

6. Bake the first tray 10–12 minutes, or until the edges start to lightly brown. Remove from oven and allow to cool completely on a wire cooling rack. Repeat with second tray of tarts.

7. To make glaze, combine powdered sugar and half-and-half and stir well to combine. Add food coloring one drop at a time and stir. Add additional drops until desired color is reached. The entire batch can be made the same color, or it can be divided into multiple bowls to make multiple colors.

8. Once tarts are fully cooled, place a spoonful of glaze on top of each tart and garnish with sprinkles, if desired. Let glaze harden prior to serving.

I bet Rarity will love these tarts—I tried to make them look nice for her!

Caramel Apple Crisp

Makes 16 servings

This apple crisp is even easier to make than pie!

Ingredients

1	cup all-purpose flour
1½	cups rolled oats (old-fashioned preferred, instant OK)
3	tsp ground cinnamon, divided
1	cup packed brown sugar
1	cup cold butter, cut into small pieces (about ¼")
½	cup shredded coconut (opt)
½	cup granulated sugar
1	Tbsp cornstarch
6–8	large apples, peeled and cubed; pieces should be under 1"
1–2	Tbsp lemon juice
½	cup caramel sauce

Directions

1. Preheat oven to 350°F.

2. In a large bowl, combine flour, oats, 1 teaspoon cinnamon and brown sugar. Cut in butter with a pastry cutter or two knives until mixture has a crumbly texture. If adding coconut, mix in at this time. Set mixture aside.

3. Grease the sides and bottom of a 13x9" baking dish.

4. In a small bowl, combine granulated sugar, 2 teaspoons cinnamon and cornstarch and mix well.

5. Place chopped and peeled apples into a large bowl. Drizzle lemon juice over apples and stir to combine. Sprinkle sugar, cinnamon and cornstarch mixture over apples and stir until well-combined.

6. Pour apple mixture into prepared pan. Top with crumb mixture.

7. Bake 45–50 minutes. Remove from oven and immediately drizzle ½ cup of caramel sauce over apple crisp, then allow to cool slightly prior to serving.

Load mine up with extra caramel sauce and ice cream!

BEST BAKING APPLES
Granny Smith, Jonagold, Golden Delicious, Honeycrisp, Jonathan, Braeburn

APPLES TO AVOID WHEN BAKING
Red Delicious, Fuji, McIntosh, Gala, Rome

Peach Crumble Pie

Makes 8 servings

You could use this topping on any fruit pie you like!

Ingredients

Crust
1   refrigerated pie crust or your favorite pie crust recipe

Filling
3   pounds fresh peaches, peeled and sliced
1   Tbsp lemon juice
¼   cup granulated sugar
2   Tbsp flour

Topping
¾   cup all-purpose flour
¾   cup old-fashioned oats
¼   tsp salt
1½   tsp cinnamon
¾   cup packed brown sugar
½   cup cold butter, cut into small pieces

I'm going to bake this pie just for Rarity!

Directions

1. Preheat oven to 350°F.

2. Press pie crust into a 9" pie dish, and shape edges as desired.

3. In a medium bowl, gently stir together peaches, lemon juice, sugar and 2 tablespoons flour. Pour mixture into the pie crust.

4. Whisk together remaining flour, oats, salt, cinnamon and brown sugar. Cut in the butter using a pastry blender or two knives until the mixture clumps together.

5. Sprinkle topping over peaches.

6. Bake 35–45 minutes, or until the top starts turning golden and crisp and the peach juice is bubbling around the edges.

7. Remove and let cool before serving. Serve with a scoop of ice cream, if desired.

Strawberry Pretzel Pie

Makes 8

Sweet strawberries and salty pretzels make for a perfect pie!

Ingredients

Pretzel Pie Crust
- 3   cups small pretzels
- 4   Tbsp brown sugar
- ½   cup unsalted butter, melted

Cheesecake Layer Pie Filling
- 8   oz cream cheese, softened
- 1   Tbsp lemon juice
- 1   tsp lemon zest
- ¼   cup sugar

- ½   cup heavy cream

Strawberry Layer Pie Filling
- 4   cups strawberries, washed and cut
- ¼   cup sugar
- ½   cup water
- 1   Tbsp lemon juice
- 3   Tbsp strawberry gelatin mix (measure straight from the box)
- 2   Tbsp cornstarch

A store-bought graham cracker pie crust will work as well.

I bet raspberries or blueberries would be tasty here, too!

Directions

1. Preheat oven to 350°F.

2. Place all piecrust ingredients into a food processor and process until the ingredients resemble the texture of wet sand.

3. Press crust mixture into the bottom and up the sides of a greased 9" pie pan.

4. Bake 10 minutes. Allow to cool completely prior to filling.

5. To make filling, in a large bowl using an electric mixer, combine cream cheese, lemon juice, lemon zest and sugar until light and fluffy.

6. In a medium bowl, beat heavy cream until stiff peaks form. Fold whipped cream into cream cheese mixture just until combined, then spread into prepared pie crust. Chill in refrigerator for 2 hours.

7. In a medium saucepan, combine sugar, water, lemon juice, dry strawberry gelatin and cornstarch. Bring to boil over medium heat and let bubble for 1 minute. Remove from heat.

8. Place cleaned and cut strawberries in a bowl, and pour strawberry glaze mixture over strawberries. Toss to coat strawberries in glaze. Spoon strawberry mixture onto cheesecake mixture. Refrigerate for at least 4 hours prior to serving.

Notes If you don't have a food processor, the pretzels can be placed in a large freezer bag and crushed with a rolling pin, then ingredients can be mixed in a bowl.

Apple Slab Pie

Makes 24 servings

This giant pie is big on flavor—and it's huge!

Ingredients

2	boxes refrigerated pie crust, softened as directed on boxes
¾	cup granulated sugar
3	Tbsp all-purpose flour
I	tsp ground cinnamon
I	tsp ground nutmeg
2	tsp cornstarch
½	tsp salt
I½	Tbsp lemon juice
8	large cored, peeled and chopped apples
I	large egg

Directions

1. Preheat oven to 400°F.

2. Open one box of pie crusts and remove the two pie crusts from their packaging. On a lightly floured surface, unroll the pie crusts and stack one on top of the other. Roll to a rectangle about 17x12". Place crust into 15x10x1" pan, pressing firmly into corners and sides. Do not trim pie crust edges.

3. In a small bowl, combine granulated sugar, flour, cinnamon, nutmeg, cornstarch, salt and lemon juice. Add apples, stirring to coat. Using a slotted spoon, gently spoon apple mixture into crust-lined pan. Only add the apples, not any juices that may be in the bowl along with the apples.

4. Open the remaining box of pie crusts. On a lightly floured surface, unroll the pie crusts and stack one on top of the other. Roll to a rectangle that is about 17x12". Place crust on top of apple mixture. Pinch edges of crusts together to seal, tucking under extra crust, if necessary. Flute or crimp edges, if desired. Cut several small slits in top crust to vent. Brush with beaten egg,

5. Bake 40–45 minutes, or until pie crust is golden brown. Remove from oven and allow to cool for at least 2 hours. Cut into squares and serve with ice cream, if desired.

This makes enough for everypony at an Apple Family reunion!

You can also use a cookie cutter to make cute vents for your pie crust! Just press the shapes out before putting the top layer of crust on your pie.

Chocolate Dream Pie

Makes 8 servings

Put a twist on this classic with colorful cream!

Ingredients

Crust
- 30   regular style Oreos® (not double-stuffed)
- 6   Tbsp butter, melted

Filling
- 12   oz semi-sweet chocolate chips
- 1½   cups heavy whipping cream, divided
- ¼   cup powdered sugar, sifted
- 1   Tbsp pure vanilla extract

Colored Whipped Cream (opt)
- 1   cup heavy whipping cream
-      Food coloring
- 3   Tbsp powdered sugar, sifted
- 4   Tbsp (approx half of a standard 4-serving box) white chocolate or vanilla instant pudding mix

Is there anything more dreamy and delicious than chocolate and cream?

Directions

1. Preheat oven to 350°F.

2. Using a food processor, pulse cookies until a fine crumb forms.

3. Mix cookie crumbs with melted butter and press crust mixture into the bottom and up the sides of a greased 9" pie pan.

4. Bake for 10 minutes and allow to cool completely prior to filing.

5. To make filling, combine chocolate chips and ¾ cup heavy whipping cream in a microwavable bowl. Microwave on high 30 seconds, then remove from microwave and stir well. Repeat heating on high for 30 seconds, then stirring well until mixture is smooth. This usually takes 90–120 seconds total. Cool mixture to room temperature.

6. Stir in powdered sugar and vanilla extract and set aside.

7. In a separate bowl beat remaining ¾ cup heavy whipping cream with an electric mixer until soft peaks form. Add ½ of the chocolate mixture to the whipped cream and beat on high until mixed. Add remaining chocolate mixture and beat on high until mixed.

8. Spoon filling into prepared pie crust and refrigerate for at least 6 hours prior to serving. If desired, top with fresh whipped cream.

9. To make colored whipped cream, pour the 1 cup of whipping cream into a 2-cup measuring cup. Add a single drop of food coloring in desired shade, and mix with a spoon. If a more intense color is desired, add an additional drop and repeat process until desired shade is reached.

10. Place powdered sugar and dry pudding mix into a **cold** mixing bowl, and pour colored whipping cream onto the powdered sugar. Beat with an electric mixer just until stiff peaks start to form. Do not over-beat or whipped cream can begin to break down.

11. Scoop or pipe with a piping bag onto pie and serve immediately.

Pudding mix is added dry. Make sure to use instant pudding mix, not cook-and-serve. Pudding mix can be left out of this recipe, but if so, whipped cream needs to be served immediately. The pudding mix helps stabilize the whipped cream so it can last longer.

If you don't have a food processor, the Oreos can be placed in a large freezer bag and crushed with a rolling pin.

73

Chocolate Chip Cookie Pie

Makes 8 servings

Combine everypony's two favorite things in one dessert!

Ingredients

2	large eggs
½	cup all-purpose flour
½	cup granulated sugar
½	cup packed light or dark brown sugar

¾	cup butter, softened
1	cup chocolate chips
1	unbaked, standard size pie crust, homemade or store-bought

Directions

1. Preheat oven to 325°F.

2. In a large bowl with an electric mixer, beat eggs until foamy.

3. Add flour and sugars to egg mixture and beat until well blended.

4. Add in softened butter and beat until blended. Stir in chocolate chips.

5. Spoon mixture into unbaked pie crust.

6. Bake for 50–55 minutes.

7. Allow to cool for at least 20 minutes prior to serving.

I like mine "à la mode." That's a fancy way of saying "with ice cream!"

Banana Chocolate
Chip Muffins, p. 86

I just love a slice of warm bread fresh from the oven!

Breads & Muffins

These bake up so nice you don't even need frosting. (But nopony would mind if you added some!)

Apple Fritter Bread

Makes 8 slices

We bet this is the best apple bread in Equestria!

Ingredients

Bread

⅓	cup packed brown sugar
2	tsp cinnamon, divided
2	medium apples, peeled and diced
⅔	cup plus 2 Tbsp sugar, divided
½	cup butter, softened
2	eggs
1½	tsp vanilla extract
1½	cups all-purpose flour
2	tsp baking powder
½	cup milk

Glaze

½	cup powdered sugar
1	Tbsp milk

Just like Granny Smith always makes!

Directions

1. Preheat oven to 350°F. Prepare a 9x5" loaf pan with nonstick cooking spray.

2. Prepare cinnamon-sugar mixture by combining brown sugar with 1 teaspoon cinnamon and mixing well until combined. Set aside.

3. Prepare apple mixture by combining apples with 2 tablespoons sugar and remaining 1 teaspoon cinnamon and mix until well-combined. Set aside.

4. In a mixing bowl, combine butter and ⅔ cup sugar and beat with an electric mixer until light and creamy, about 2–3 minutes. Beat in eggs one at a time until well-blended. Add vanilla and beat until blended.

5. Add flour and baking powder to mixture and stir by hand until well-blended. Add milk to mixture and stir until combined, but do not overmix.

6. Pour half the batter into the prepared bread pan. Distribute half of the apple mixture over the batter. Sprinkle half the cinnamon-sugar mixture over the apples. Using the end of a dull knife, gently swirl the brown sugar mixture and apples into the batter. Pour remaining batter into bread pan, followed by remaining apple mixture, then remaining cinnamon-sugar mixture. Gently swirl the brown sugar mixture and apples into the batter. If needed, gently press the apples into the batter.

7. Bake in preheated oven for 50–60 minutes, or until a toothpick inserted into the center comes out clean. Allow to cool in pan for 10–15 minutes, then gently run a knife around the edges of the bread pan to help loosen the loaf. Invert and remove from the pan.

8. To make glaze, combine powdered sugar and milk (or cream) until well-combined. Drizzle over bread.

Iced Lemon Loaf

Makes 10 servings

Serve with berries for a delicious dessert or snack!

Ingredients

Loaf
½ cup butter, at room temperature
1 cup granulated sugar
3 large eggs, at room temperature
2 Tbsp lemon zest (from about 1 large lemon)
1 Tbsp lemon juice
2 tsp vanilla
1½ cups all-purpose flour
¼ tsp salt
¼ tsp baking soda
¼ tsp baking powder
⅓ cup sour cream

Glaze
½ cup powdered sugar
1 Tbsp lemon juice, plus more as needed

Directions

1. Preheat oven to 325°F. Spray an 8x4" loaf pan with nonstick cooking spray, then place a piece of parchment paper into the pan. The ends of the parchment paper should be long enough for you to easily lift out the loaf after baking.

2. In a large bowl, use an electric mixer to beat the butter and sugar until light and fluffy, about 3 minutes. Add the eggs one at a time and beat in well after each addition, scraping down the sides of the bowl as needed. Add lemon zest, lemon juice and vanilla and mix well to combine.

3. In a separate bowl, mix together flour, salt, baking soda and baking powder.

4. Add ⅓ of the flour mixture to the butter mixture and mix on low until combined. Add half the sour cream and mix on low until combined. Repeat the process, then mix in the rest of the flour mixture.

5. Scoop the batter into prepared loaf pan. Bake for 55–60 minutes, or until a toothpick inserted in the center comes out clean.

6. Allow loaf to cool in the pan for 15 minutes, then gently run a knife along the sides of the pan to help loosen the loaf from the pan. Next, use the edges of the parchment paper to lift and remove from pan. Allow to cool on a cooling rack.

7. Prepare the glaze by mixing together powdered sugar and lemon juice. If a thinner glaze is desired, additional lemon juice can be added 1 teaspoon at a time. Place the loaf on a tray (to catch any drips) and gently pour glaze over loaf.

8. Allow to cool completely prior to serving.

This lemon loaf is simple yet fabulous!

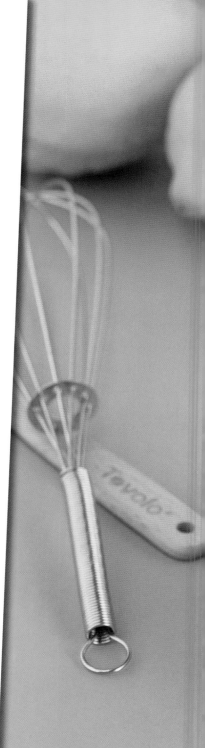

Carrot Zucchini Bread

Makes 10 slices   **Nopony will believe this bread is full of veggies!**

Ingredients

Bread
- 1½ cups all-purpose flour
- 1 tsp baking powder
- ½ tsp baking soda
- ½ tsp salt
- 1 tsp ground cinnamon
- ¼ tsp ground nutmeg
- ½ cup granulated sugar
- ¼ cup packed light brown sugar
- ¼ cup canola or vegetable oil
- 3 Tbsp unsweetened applesauce
- 2 large eggs
- 1 tsp vanilla extract
- ¾ cup peeled, finely shredded carrots (from about 2 medium carrots)
- ¾ cup finely shredded zucchini (from about 1 small zucchini)

Frosting (opt)
- 3 Tbsp butter, softened
- 3 oz cream cheese, softened
- 1½ cups powdered sugar
- ¼ tsp salt
- ½ tsp vanilla extract

> I just know Angel will love munching on this!

Directions

1. Preheat oven to 350°F. Butter and lightly flour an 8x4" loaf pan. Set aside.

2. In a large bowl, mix together flour, baking powder, baking soda, salt, cinnamon and nutmeg until well-combined.

3. In a separate large bowl, mix together granulated sugar and brown sugar until well-combined. Add oil, applesauce, eggs and vanilla and mix until well-combined (approximately 1 minute).

4. Add shredded carrots, zucchini and flour mixture to the wet mixture and mix just until combined. Do not overmix.

5. Pour mixture into prepared 8x4" pan. Bake for 35 minutes, then carefully place a sheet of aluminum foil over the top of the loaf pan without removing the pan from the oven, in order to prevent over browning. Continue to bake for an additional 15–20 minutes, or until toothpick inserted into center of loaf comes out clean.

6. Remove from oven and allow to cool in loaf pan for 5 minutes, then invert onto a wire rack and cool completely. If desired, frost with frosting once bread has cooled.

7. To make optional frosting, place softened butter and softened cream cheese into a mixing bowl. Using an electric mixer, beat together butter and cream cheese until smooth and fluffy. Add powdered sugar, salt and vanilla and continue to mix on medium speed until light and fluffy, about 3 minutes.

Canterlot Cornbread

Makes 16 servings

Serve this cornbread with dinner and everypony will come running!

Ingredients

1	cup cornmeal	⅔	cup vegetable oil
3	cups all-purpose flour	⅓	cup melted butter
1⅓	cups sugar	2	Tbsp honey
2	Tbsp baking powder	4	eggs, beaten
1	tsp salt	2½	cups whole milk

Directions

1. Preheat oven to 350°F and grease a 9x13" baking dish.

2. Mix together the cornmeal, flour, sugar, baking powder and salt in a mixing bowl. Add in vegetable oil, melted butter, honey, beaten eggs and milk, and stir until combined, but do not overmix.

3. Pour the batter into the prepared baking dish and bake for about 45 minutes, or until the top of the cornbread starts to brown and show cracks.

The best way to eat this is with butter and honey!

Banana Chocolate Chip Muffins

Makes 12 muffins

These tasty muffins are the perfect treat for dessert—or even breakfast!

Ingredients

3	very ripe large bananas	1½	cups all-purpose flour
¾	cup granulated sugar	1	tsp baking powder
1	egg, lightly beaten	½	tsp salt
⅓	cup melted butter	1	cup mini chocolate chips

If desired, ½ cup of chopped nuts can be added with the chocolate chips.

These would be great with a scoop of banana brickle ice cream!

Directions

1. Preheat oven to 350°F. Prepare a muffin pan with 12 paper muffin liners.

2. In a large bowl, mash bananas until no large lumps remain.

3. Add sugar and lightly beaten egg to banana mixture and stir to combine.

4. Add melted butter to mixture and stir to combine.

5. Add flour, baking powder and salt, and stir until just combined.

6. Gently stir in chocolate chips.

7. Divide batter among 12 cups in muffin pan.

8. Bake for 18–22 minutes, or until a toothpick inserted into the center of a muffin comes out clean.

9. Remove from oven and allow to slightly cool prior to serving.

Double Chocolate Muffins

Makes 16 servings

These are best shared with everypony who loves chocolate!

Dark cocoa powder, such as Hershey's Special Dark, works great in this recipe.

Ingredients

1	egg
1	cup plain unflavored yogurt
¾	cup milk
1	tsp vanilla extract
½	cup vegetable oil
2	cups all-purpose flour
1	cup granulated sugar
½	cup mini chocolate chips (standard size chocolate chips work as well)
½	cup unsweetened cocoa powder
¼	tsp salt
1	tsp baking soda

Directions

1. Preheat oven to 400°F. Line muffin tins with 16 paper muffin liners.

2. In a large bowl, whisk egg, yogurt, milk, vanilla and vegetable oil until smooth.

3. Add flour, sugar, chocolate chips, cocoa powder, salt and baking soda.

4. Scoop mixture into prepared muffin cups, about ⅔ full in each muffin cup.

5. Bake in preheated oven until a toothpick inserted into the center comes out clean, about 15–19 minutes. Cool in the pans for 10 minutes before removing to cool completely on a wire rack.

I love this recipe because it makes enough for all my friends!

Unflavored Greek yogurt is a great choice in this recipe and gives your muffins extra protein. Because it is thicker than regular yogurt, increase milk by ¼ cup if using Greek yogurt.

Pumpkin Apple Muffins

Makes 12 Muffins

These muffins are perfect for fall, but you can make them any time of year.

Ingredients

2	cups all-purpose flour
1	tsp baking soda
1	tsp baking powder
1	tsp cinnamon
2	tsp pumpkin pie spice
1	tsp salt
½	cup sugar
½	cup packed brown sugar
1	cup canned pumpkin (not pumpkin pie mix)
½	cup unsweetened applesauce
⅓	cup apple juice (water can be used as well)
2	eggs
1½	cups finely chopped or grated apples
	Opt: 1 cup chopped nuts, such as walnuts or pecans

I hope these will give Rainbow Dash tons of energy for her morning trainings!

Directions

1. Preheat oven to 350°F. Prepare a muffin pan with 12 paper muffin liners.

2. Place dry ingredients into a large bowl and stir well to combine.

3. In a separate bowl, combine pumpkin, applesauce, apple juice and eggs, and mix well to combine. Add liquid mixture to dry ingredient mixture and stir until combined, but do not overmix. Fold in chopped/grated apple and chopped nuts, if using.

4. Scoop into prepared muffin pan.

5. Bake for about 15 minutes, or until a toothpick inserted into the center of a muffin comes out clean.

6. Remove from oven and allow to cool.

Baking these cakes is going to be totally awesome!

Cakes & Cupcakes

It's not a party without some kind of cake!

Piñata Cupcakes,
p. 102

Lemon Cupcakes

Makes 12 cupcakes

These lemon cupcakes are so light and sweet, they'll fly off the plate!

Gilda the Griffon is going to love these!

Ingredients

Cupcakes
2½	cups all-purpose flour
2½	tsp baking powder
¼	tsp salt
½	cup butter, softened
1¾	cups sugar
2	large eggs, at room temperature
1¼	cups whole milk, at room temperature
1	tsp vanilla extract

1	tsp lemon extract
½	cup freshly squeezed lemon juice
2	Tbsp freshly grated lemon zest

Frosting
4	Tbsp butter, softened
6	oz cream cheese, at room temperature
4	cups powdered sugar
1	tsp vanilla extract
1	tsp lemon extract

Directions

1. Preheat oven to 350°F. Line a standard cupcake pan with 12 paper cupcake liners.

2. In a medium bowl, mix together flour, baking powder and salt.

3. In a large bowl with an electric mixer, cream together the butter and sugar until light and fluffy, about 2–3 minutes. Add the eggs one at a time, mixing slowly after each addition.

4. Add half of the dry ingredients followed by half of the milk, and mix thoroughly. Add vanilla and lemon extracts and mix thoroughly.

5. Add remaining half of the dry ingredients and mix until combined. Add remaining milk and mix slowly until just incorporated. Add lemon juice and zest, and gently mix until well-combined.

6. Scoop the batter into the cupcake pan using a standard size ice cream scoop. Each cupcake cavity should be about two-thirds of the way full.

7. Bake for 15–18 minutes, or until a toothpick inserted into the center of a cupcake comes out clean.

8. Transfer the pan to a wire rack to cool completely prior to frosting.

9. To make frosting, combine the ingredients in a large bowl and mix well until light and airy, about 2–3 minutes. Frost cupcakes with an offset spatula, or pipe frosting on with a piping bag.

To make the strawberry purée, place about 16 ounces of frozen strawberries into a large bowl to thaw (this may take a few hours). Once thawed, place strawberries and their juice into the bowl of a food processor or blender and process until smooth. You can also cut the strawberries into tiny pieces and mash with a fork until as smooth as possible.

Strawberry Cupcakes

Makes 24 cupcakes

These fruity cupcakes are always a hit!

Ingredients

Cupcakes

1	standard size pkg vanilla cake mix
1	(approx 3-oz) pkg strawberry Jell-O
¼	cup strawberry purée
4	large eggs
½	cup vegetable oil
¼	cup water

¾	cup cream cheese, softened (do not use light or nonfat cream cheese)
¾	cup butter, softened
6	cups powdered sugar
¼	cup strawberry purée
1	tsp vanilla extract
¼	cup strawberry jam

I just love a cupcake covered in berries!

Directions

1. Preheat your oven to 350°F. Line 24 muffin cups with cupcake liners.

2. Place all cupcake ingredients into a large mixing bowl and mix well with an electric mixer for 2–3 minutes.

3. Fill cupcake liners ⅔ of the way full with cupcake batter.

4. Bake 14–16 minutes, or until a toothpick inserted into the center comes out clean. Remove from oven and allow to cool completely prior to frosting.

5. To make this frosting, beat together butter and cream cheese until light and smooth, approximately 2-3 minutes, Add the powdered sugar, 1 cup at a time, until well combined.

6. Add strawberry puree, vanilla extract and jam to the mixture and mix until well combined. If frosting is too thin, add more powdered sugar (¼ cup at a time) or more strawberry puree (1 tbsp at a time) until desired consistency is reached.

Confetti Cupcakes

Makes 12 cupcakes

It's always a party when you have these colorful cupcakes!

If needed, see cake flour and buttermilk substitutions on page 13.

I would love to put these in my party cannon!

Ingredients

Cupcakes

1½	cups cake flour
¼	tsp baking soda
¾	tsp baking powder
½	tsp salt
2	large eggs, at room temperature
1	tsp pure vanilla extract
⅔	cup granulated sugar
6	Tbsp butter, melted

and slightly cooled
⅔	cup buttermilk
½	cup assorted sprinkles

Frosting

1	cup butter, softened
4½	cups powdered sugar
¼	cup heavy whipping cream
2	tsp pure vanilla extract

Directions

1. Preheat oven to 325°F. Line a cupcake pan with 12 paper liners.

2. Whisk together cake flour, baking soda, baking powder and salt in a bowl and set aside.

3. In a separate bowl, whisk together eggs and vanilla until well-blended. Whisk in sugar until well-blended. Slowly whisk in butter and mix well to combine.

4. Add half the dry mixture to the wet mixture and mix until combined. Mix in the buttermilk and stir until combined. Mix in remaining dry mixture and mix just until combined.

5. Gently fold in sprinkles and mix just until combined. Overmixing will result in the sprinkle colors bleeding into the cake batter.

6. Scoop batter into prepared cupcake liners. Each should be about ⅔-full.

7. Bake for 18–22 minutes, or until a toothpick inserted into the center comes out clean. Remove from oven and allow to completely cool prior to frosting.

8. To make frosting, beat butter until light and creamy, about 3 minutes.

9. Add powdered sugar to the butter mixture and mix until combined. Add in heavy cream and vanilla extract. Once combined, mix 2–3 minutes on high speed. If frosting is too thin, add more powdered sugar, 1 tablespoon at a time. If frosting is too thick, add more heavy cream, 1 teaspoon at a time, until desired consistency is reached.

10. Spread or pipe frosting onto cooled cupcakes. Decorate with sprinkles.

Jimmies-style sprinkles work best in this recipe. Nonpareil sprinkles tend to bleed their colors almost immediately, distorting the "confetti" effect.

Cupcake Cones

Makes 24 servings

Surprise everypony with these cones that will never melt!

Ingredients

Cupcake Cones
1   standard-sized cake mix in flavor of your choice, along with ingredients called for on pkg

24   flat-bottom ice cream cones

Frosting
2   cups unsalted butter, at room temperature

5   cups powdered sugar

2   Tbsp vanilla extract

Directions

1. Preheat oven to 350°F.

2. Prepare cake mix according to package directions. Scoop about 3 Tbsp of cake batter into each cone, filling ½–⅔ of the cone.

3. Carefully stand cones with batter upright in a muffin tin and gently place into the oven. The cones can be a bit unsteady, so be very careful to place them in the oven upright.

4. Bake 22–26 minutes, or until toothpick carefully inserted in center comes out clean.

Allow to cool completely, about 1 hour.

5. To make frosting, beat butter with an electric mixer for 3–5 minutes, or until very light and fluffy. Add powdered sugar and mix on low until well-combined, then mix on medium for 1–2 minutes. Add in vanilla and mix until combined.

6. Using a piping bag, pipe frosting onto the top of each cupcake. Decorate with sprinkles and candies, if desired.

To make a rainbow of frosting on your cupcakes, separate frosting into 2-3 separate bowls and use food coloring to color each as desired. Carefully scoop each color into one piping bag, putting one color to each side and being careful not to mix. Pipe on as usual!

What a wonderful treat to share with friends!

To make multi-colored cupcake cones, separate batter into bowls and color individually. Carefully spoon the batter into the cones, and don't stir!

Piñata Cupcakes

Makes 24 servings

Break open these fun cakes to see what's inside!

Ingredients

Cupcakes

2	cups sugar
1¾	cups all-purpose flour
¾	cup cocoa powder (natural, not Dutch process)
1½	tsp baking powder
1½	tsp baking soda
1	tsp salt
2	eggs
1	cup milk
½	cup vegetable oil
2	tsp vanilla extract
1	cup water, boiling
½–1	cup assorted sprinkles or small candies

Frosting

1	cup butter, melted
1⅓	cups unsweetened cocoa powder
6	cups powdered sugar
⅔	cup heavy cream or milk
2	tsp pure vanilla extract

Directions

1. Heat oven to 350°F. Line 24 muffin cups with standard sized cupcake liners.

2. Mix together sugar, flour, cocoa, baking powder, baking soda and salt in large bowl.

3. Add eggs, milk, oil and vanilla, and beat on medium speed of mixer for 2 minutes. Carefully stir in boiling water. The batter will be quite thin. Fill prepared cups two-thirds full with batter.

4. Bake 22–25 minutes, or until wooden toothpick inserted in centers comes out clean. Cool completely in pans on a wire cooling rack.

5. Once cupcakes are completely cool, have an adult help to use a knife to cut a hole about 1" in diameter and 1" deep into the center of each cupcake. Using the knife, gently lift the center piece out of the cupcake after cutting. Cut the bottom off each center piece (these make a great mid-baking snack!) and set the tops aside, to be placed back onto cupcakes after filling.

6. Pack the center of your cupcake with filling of your choice, such as assorted sprinkles or small candies such as mini M&M's®, rainbow chips or other small candies. Fill almost to the top of the cupcake. Place the tops back onto the cupcakes to "plug" the hole filled with your filling.

7. To make frosting, once butter is melted, stir in cocoa and mix until butter and cocoa have combined.

8. Using an electric mixer, alternately add powdered sugar and cream, beating until light and fluffy. Add vanilla and mix well.

9. Add an extra teaspoon of cream if a thinner consistency is desired. If frosting seems too thin, add additional powdered sugar 1 tablespoon at a time until desired consistency is reached.

10. Spread or pipe onto cupcakes as desired.

I love this recipe—you get to taste-test your cake before it's done!

See frosting tips on page 20!

Purple Velvet Cake

Makes 16 slices

This velvety smooth cake can be colored any way you like!

Ingredients

Cake
1½ cups butter, softened

3 cups granulated sugar

5 large eggs, room temperature

3 cups all-purpose flour

2 tsp baking powder

¼ tsp salt

½ cup whole milk, room temperature

½ cup buttermilk, room temperature

2 tsp vanilla extract
Purple food coloring (any other color may be used as well)

Frosting
2 cups white buttercream frosting, store-bought or homemade (p. 20)

Directions

1. Preheat oven to 350°F. Prepare three 9" round cake pans with nonstick cooking spray, or coat them well with butter and a dusting of flour to prevent cakes from sticking.

2. Cream the butter with an electric mixer until light and fluffy, for at least 3–5 minutes. Add sugar 1 cup at a time, making sure each cup is fully mixed in before adding the next cup. Add eggs, one at a time, making sure to fully incorporate each egg before adding another, but careful not to over-beat.

3. Mix together flour, baking powder and salt. Pour milk, buttermilk and vanilla into measuring cup and whisk together to combine. Add ⅓ flour mixture to butter mixture followed by half of milk mixture. Do not stir. Repeat until all ingredients are in mixing bowl.

4. Gently stir all ingredients until well-combined. Make sure to stop mixing and scrape down sides of the bowl at least once to ensure all ingredients are thoroughly mixed.

5. Mix three drops food coloring into batter just until combined. Additional food coloring can be added to achieve the desired color, but do not overmix.

6. Pour batter into cake pans. Bake 25–30 minutes, or until a toothpick inserted in the center comes out clean. Remove and allow to cool slightly in cake pans for about 5 minutes. Carefully run a knife along the pan's edges, and remove cake by inverting it. Allow to cool for 20 minutes more on the wire rack right-side up. Make sure to allow cake to cool completely prior to frosting.

I didn't know velvet could taste as good as it looks!

Magic Mix Cake

Makes 16 servings

This cake is full of magical possibilities!

Ingredients

1	box (15–17 oz) cake mix (white/vanilla cake mix if a colored cake is desired)
1	pkg (3–4 oz) instant pudding mix (do not use "cook and serve" or sugar-free)
1	cup full-fat sour cream
1	cup vegetable or canola oil
4	large eggs
½	cup milk
1	tsp vanilla extract
¼	tsp salt
	Food coloring (opt)
	Best Buttercream Frosting (see p. 21)

I'll study this cake's magical properties... after I finish eating it!

This recipe really is like magic! Many different flavors of cakes and puddings can be used. Chocolate cake mix + chocolate pudding; vanilla cake mix + vanilla pudding; lemon cake mix + lemon pudding; strawberry cake mix + cheesecake pudding—get creative and try different delicious combinations!

Directions

1. Preheat oven according to directions on cake mix package. Prepare three 9" round cake pans with nonstick cooking spray, or coat them well with butter and a dusting of flour to prevent cakes from sticking.

2. Combine all ingredients in a mixing bowl and mix with an electric mixer until all ingredients are well-combined.

3. If desired, the batter of a white or vanilla cake mix can be colored. For a single cake color, simply add food coloring to the bowl with the batter.

   For multiple colors, divide batter among three bowls evenly and add food coloring to each bowl. Mix well to combine.

4. Pour batter into prepared cake pans. Bake according to layer cake directions on the box.

5. Remove and allow to cool slightly in cake pans for about 5 minutes, then invert cakes to remove from pan and allow to cool completely on a wire rack. Make sure to allow cake to cool completely prior to frosting.

For a six-layer cake as pictured here, make two batches of this recipe to create six cake layers, and double the frosting recipe on p. 20. Stacking six layers can be quite a challenge, so practice with plenty of three-layer cakes first!

Chocolate Lava Cakes

Makes 2 servings　　**Double or triple this recipe to make enough for everypony!**

Ingredients

¼	cup butter	½	tsp vanilla extract
2	oz semi-sweet chocolate, chopped	¼	cup all-purpose flour
½	cup powdered sugar		Additional butter and flour to grease and prep ramekins
1	large egg		
1	egg yolk		

How do you make chocolate cake better? You add a chocolate explosion inside!

Directions

1. Preheat oven to 425°F. Very thoroughly grease the inside of two 6-ounce ramekins with butter, then sprinkle lightly with a small amount of all-purpose flour, tapping out any excess flour. Place on a baking sheet and set aside.

2. Add the butter and semi-sweet chocolate to a large microwavable bowl and microwave for 30 seconds. Remove and stir well for 1 minute. If not all chocolate pieces have melted, heat for an additional 10 seconds and mix again. Repeat until chocolate and butter mixture is smooth.

3. Whisk in powdered sugar until well-combined, then add in the egg, egg yolk and vanilla and mix until fully combined.

4. Add in the flour and mix until just combined—don't overmix the batter. Divide the batter between the two prepared ramekins.

5. Bake at 425°F for 12–14 minutes, or until the edges are firm and the center is just slightly soft.

6. Remove from the oven and allow to stand for 1 minute. Have an adult carefully invert each very hot ramekin onto a small plate. Serve immediately as is, or top with ice cream, whipped cream, powdered sugar or fruit.

Rainbow Bundt Cake

Makes 12 servings   Cut into this cake to reveal a colorful ponypiece!

Ingredients

Cake
1	standard size box white or vanilla cake mix
1	(3.4-oz) pkg vanilla instant pudding (dry mix, unprepared)
1	cup full-fat sour cream
1	cup vegetable oil
4	eggs
½	cup warm water Food coloring—red, orange, yellow, green, blue and purple

Glaze
2	cups powdered sugar
2	Tbsp milk
1	tsp vanilla extract

Directions

1. Preheat oven to 350°F.

2. Combine all cake ingredients and mix with a mixer until combined. Do not overmix, but make sure all dry ingredients and wet ingredients are well-combined.

3. Divide cake batter evenly between six bowls.

4. For each bowl, add 1–2 drops of food coloring and mix. If more color is desired, add additional drops of food coloring until desired color is reached. Repeat with each bowl.

5. Generously spray a standard sized Bundt cake pan with nonstick cooking spray.

6. Starting with the red batter, spoon cake batter into bottom of pan. The cake batter should go around the bottom of the pan in a complete circle.

7. Carefully spoon the orange cake batter into pan, placing it directly on the red cake batter, once again making sure it goes completely around the red cake batter. Try not to mix the different colored cake batters; simply spoon one on top of the other. Repeat with remaining colors in the following order: yellow, green, blue, purple.

8. Place in oven and bake for 50–55 minutes, or until toothpick inserted into cake comes out clean.

9. Remove from oven and allow to cool in pan, on a wire rack, for 10–15 minutes.

10. Tap the pan firmly a few times on the countertop, gently shaking it to help loosen the cake. Carefully invert the pan onto a cake plate and lift the pan off of the cake. Allow the cake to cool completely prior to adding glaze.

11. To make glaze, place powdered sugar and milk into a bowl and stir well to combine. Add vanilla and stir to combine. Glaze should be thin enough to spoon over cake, but not runny. If glaze is too thick, add additional milk, one teaspoon at a time, until a spoonable consistency is reached.

12. Spoon glaze over the top of cake.

13. If desired, garnish with rainbow sprinkles.

This is probably the best looking cake in Equestria!

This cake is shown in a classic rainbow, but you can get creative and use any combination of colors!

111

Pony Poke Cake

Makes 16 servings

Use any combination of colors you like to make this cake your own!

Ingredients

Cake

1	cup butter, softened
2⅓	cups sugar
5	egg whites
1	Tbsp pure vanilla extract
½	tsp salt
4	tsp baking powder
3	cups all-purpose flour
1½	cups room temperature milk (2 percent or whole milk works best)
3	bottles food coloring in complementary colors
1	can sweetened condensed milk

Frosting

1	cup butter, softened
4	cups powdered sugar
2	tsp pure vanilla extract
¼	tsp salt
4–6	Tbsp heavy whipping cream or milk

Directions

1. Preheat oven to 350°F.

2. Using a mixer, cream the butter and sugar until light and fluffy, about 2–3 minutes.

3. Add in egg whites and vanilla, and mix until well-combined.

4. In a separate bowl, combine salt, baking powder and flour. Stir to combine.

5. Add half of the dry ingredients to the butter mixture and mix to combine. Add in milk and mix to combine. Add in remaining dry ingredients and mix until combined.

6. Divide batter evenly between three bowls. Add 2–3 drops of food coloring to each bowl and mix well. Additional drops of food coloring can be added, until desired colors are reached.

7. Spoon each of the colored batters into a 13x9" pan that has been sprayed with nonstick cooking oil. Different colored batters should touch and can mix slightly, but avoid stirring colors while adding them to maintain the distinct colors in the cake.

8. Bake 30–35 minutes, or until the center of the cake springs back when lightly touched and a toothpick inserted into the center comes out clean.

9. Using a straw or the back of a spoon, poke about 24 small holes into the cake. Pour sweetened condensed milk over the cake and into the holes. Allow cake to cool completely prior to frosting.

10. To make frosting, with a mixer, beat butter until light and fluffy, about 2–3 minutes.

11. Add powdered sugar and mix until well-combined. Add in vanilla and salt and mix until combined.

12. Add 4 tablespoons of cream or milk and mix until very well-combined, about 2 minutes. If a thinner frosting is desired, add additional cream or milk until desired consistency is reached.

13. Spread frosting over cooled cake. Decorate with sprinkles, if desired.

This cake is a favorite for every cowpoke on my apple farm!

Cake Pops

Makes about 24 cake pops

Everypony's favorite bite-sized treat!

Ingredients

1	standard size cake mix, any flavor
3	eggs
1	cup water
½	cup vegetable oil
½	cup frosting, store-bought or homemade (do not use "whipped" style frosting) in any flavor that complements cake
24	oz candy melts or almond bark (not regular chocolate)
	Sprinkles (lightweight sugars, nonpareils or small quins work best)
24	lollipop sticks
	Craft block or cake pop stand to hold cake pops as they set up

Directions

1. Preheat oven to 350°F. Spray a 13x9" baking pan with nonstick cooking spray. Set aside.

2. In a large bowl combine cake mix, eggs, water and vegetable oil. Beat on medium speed with an electric mixer for 2 minutes. Pour into prepared pan.

3. Bake for about 30 minutes, or until a toothpick inserted into the center of the cake comes out clean. Cool in pan for 15 minutes.

4. Once cake is cool, crumble cake into a large bowl and combine cake crumb with frosting. This will require using your hands.

5. Form mixture into cake balls, approximately 1" in diameter. Place cake balls onto a baking sheet and place in refrigerator for 2 hours, or freezer for 20 minutes.

6. Melt candy melts according to package directions.

7. Working with one cake pop at a time, dip the tip of a lollipop stick into the melted candy melts, and then into the cake ball. Make sure the stick is secure in the cake ball. Place cake pop back on baking sheet to set up and repeat process with remaining ingredients.

8. Again working with one cake pop at a time, dip cake pops into melted candy melts. If needed, use a spoon to help coat the cake melts over the cake pop. Tap stick very gently on side of bowl to help remove excess candy melt mixture. Not too hard or the cake pop will fall off the stick! Immediately add a light coating of sprinkles.

9. Place cake pop stick into craft block or cake pop stand and allow to sit for at least 20 minutes to set up. Repeat process with remaining cake pops.

I like to make sure each cake pop looks just perfect!

Berry Baked
Oatmeal, p. 128

Y'all gonna need a hearty breakfast to get your day started!

Breakfast Favorites

The most tasty recipes for the most important meal of the day!

Celebration Cinnamon Rolls

Makes 12 cinnamon rolls **There's nothing like a hot, homemade cinnamon roll!**

Ingredients

Rolls

¾	cup hot whole milk (about 110°F)
1	packet (2¼ tsp) rapid rise or instant yeast
3	large eggs, at room temperature
4¼	cups all-purpose flour
½	cup cornstarch
½	cup sugar
1½	tsp salt
12	Tbsp butter, cut into 12 pieces and softened

Filling

1½	cups packed light or dark brown sugar
1½	Tbsp cinnamon
¼	tsp salt
1	Tbsp cornstarch
4	Tbsp softened butter

Glaze

½	cup cream cheese, softened
¼	cup butter, softened
2	tsp vanilla extract
2	cups powdered sugar
	Pinch of salt
2	Tbsp sprinkles

Directions

1. Preheat oven to 200°F, then turn off. Generously butter a 13x9" pan.

2. Combine hot milk and yeast in a bowl or measuring cup until the yeast dissolves, then whisk in eggs.

3. In the bowl of a stand mixer fitted with a dough hook, combine flour, cornstarch, sugar and salt. With mixer on low, add hot milk mixture in a steady stream and continue mixing until dough comes together, which should take about 1 minute.

4. Continue to mix dough on low until dough pulls away from the sides of the bowl and the texture becomes smooth, about 10 minutes.

5. Sprinkle a work surface with flour, then place dough on floured work surface. Knead into a smooth, round ball.

6. Place dough into a large, greased oven-proof bowl. Cover dough, in bowl, with plastic wrap. Place into oven (which is warm but turned OFF) and allow to rise until doubled in size, about 2 hours.

7. To make filling, combine brown sugar, cinnamon, salt and cornstarch in a bowl.

8. Turn dough onto a lightly floured countertop or work surface. Roll dough into a large square (about 18").

9. Spread 4 tablespoons of soft butter over the dough with pastry brush or rubber spatula. Sprinkle filling evenly over the dough and gently pat filling into dough.

10. Starting with the side nearest to you, roll the dough up tightly and cut into 12 pieces. Tip: Cut dough in half, then into quarters, then each quarter into thirds.

11. Transfer pieces to prepared 13x9" pan. Cover with plastic wrap, place in a warm spot and allow to rise until doubled in size, about 45 minutes. Preheat oven to 350°F.

12. Discard plastic wrap from buns and place into preheated oven, baking until golden brown with the centers of rolls puffing up, about 30–35 minutes. Remove from oven.

13. To make glaze, while rolls are baking, beat together softened cream cheese, butter, vanilla, powdered sugar and salt in a large bowl with an electric mixer until smooth.

14. When rolls come out of oven, immediately spread glaze over the rolls, allowing glaze to seep into the rolls. Garnish with sprinkles.

I get up super early to make these whenever there's something to celebrate!

Use a kitchen thermometer to make sure the milk is between 100-110°F. Otherwise, the yeast may not be activated and the rolls won't rise.

119

Wonderbolt French Toast

Makes 12 servings

Make this for early morning training—or for the morning after a sleepover!

Ingredients

Toast

1	large loaf of bread (bakery French or sourdough work well)
8	eggs
2	cups whole milk
½	cup heavy cream
½	cup sugar
½	cup brown sugar
¼	tsp cinnamon
2	Tbsp vanilla extract

Toppings

½	cup all-purpose flour
½	cup brown sugar
¼	tsp salt
1	tsp cinnamon
½	cup of butter, cut into small pieces and kept cold

Directions

1. Grease a 9x13" baking pan with butter.

2. Cut or tear bread into chunks, about 1" in diameter, and spread over the bottom of prepared pan.

3. In a large bowl, combine eggs, milk, cream, sugars, cinnamon and vanilla and mix until well-combined. Pour evenly over bread.

4. Tightly cover pan and place in the refrigerator overnight.

5. To make toppings, combine flour, sugar, salt and cinnamon in a bowl and mix until combined. Using two forks, a pastry cutter or food processor, add in the small pieces of cold butter and mix until ingredients are combined into small, pea sized pieces. Place mixture into a freezer storage bag, seal and place in refrigerator until ready to use.

6. Preheat oven to 350°F.

7. Remove casserole from fridge and evenly sprinkle the topping mixture over the top of it. Bake for 50–60 minutes. If top starts to brown too much, cover with foil.

8. Serve warm with syrup and fruit.

This is ALWAYS a hit at Wonderbolt practice!

Best served the same day as made.

Apple Cider Donuts

Makes 6 donuts   You'll fall so hard for these delicious donuts!

Ingredients

Donuts
3	Tbsp butter
⅓	cup apple cider
1	cup all-purpose flour
1	tsp baking powder
¼	tsp salt
¼	tsp cinnamon
¼	tsp nutmeg
¼	cup sugar

2	Tbsp honey
2	Tbsp plain sour cream
1	large egg, beaten

Topping
3	Tbsp butter
¼	cup apple cider
⅓	cup sugar
1½	tsp cinnamon

Tools
6-cavity donut pan

After a long day in the orchard, I eat these with some hot apple cider!

No donut pan? You can make these as mini muffins, baking for about 9 minutes.

Directions

1. Preheat oven to 400°F. Spray donut pan with nonstick cooking spray.

2. In a medium-sized microwavable bowl, melt butter 30 seconds at a time until fully melted. Remove from microwave and pour in apple cider. Set aside to cool for at least 5 minutes.

3. In a large bowl, mix together flour, baking powder, salt, cinnamon and nutmeg.

4. Add sugar, honey, sour cream and beaten egg to the melted butter mixture and stir until combined.

5. Add wet ingredients to dry ingredients and stir until just combined. Do not overmix.

6. Transfer batter to a piping bag or large freezer bag, snip off a bottom corner and pipe batter into donut pan cavities.

7. Bake 7–8 minutes and remove from oven. Allow donuts to sit in pan 1–2 minutes, then invert donuts onto a wire cooling rack.

8. To make topping, in a small bowl, melt butter and combine with apple cider. In a separate bowl, combine sugar and cinnamon mixture.

9. Working quickly, dip each donut into the butter mixture to cover with butter, then immediately dip in the sugar and cinnamon mixture to coat. Place back on cooling rack to finish cooling.

Princess Pancakes

Make a breakfast fit for royalty!

Makes 6 servings

Ingredients

2	cups buttermilk
2	large eggs, beaten
1	tsp vanilla extract
4	Tbsp melted butter, divided
2¼	cups all-purpose flour
¼	cup sugar
2½	tsp baking powder
1	tsp baking soda
½	tsp salt
	Your choice of berries, syrup, butter, whipped cream or powdered sugar for topping

This is my favorite way to make sure there's enough pancakes for everypony!

Directions

1. Preheat oven to 425°F.

2. Line a rimmed 11x17" baking sheet with parchment paper. Generously coat the parchment paper and the sides of the pan with nonstick cooking spray. Set aside.

3. In a large bowl, combine buttermilk, eggs, vanilla and 2 tablespoons melted butter and mix until well-combined.

4. In a separate bowl, combine flour, sugar, baking powder, baking soda and salt, and mix until well-combined.

5. Add the liquid mixture to the dry mixture and mix until just combined, but do not overmix. Batter may be slightly lumpy.

6. Spoon batter onto the prepared baking sheet and smooth into an even layer using a spatula.

7. Bake 11–13 minutes, or until the pancake starts to turn lightly golden and the center springs back when touched. Remove from oven and turn on broiler to low (or if your oven just has a broil setting, that's fine). Taking care not to touch the hot pan, brush the remaining 2 tablespoons melted butter over the pancake, then return to the oven. Broil 1–2 minutes, or until it starts to turn golden brown.

8. Remove from oven, cut and serve with your choice of toppings.

It's important to not walk away while broiling food. The broiler can work incredibly fast. To avoid burning, make sure to keep an eye on it the entire time your pancake is in the oven so you can take it out immediately when ready.

Good Morning Granola

Makes 6 servings

Make a batch the night before so you can wake up to a tasty treat!

Ingredients

3½ cups old-fashioned rolled oats
½ cup honey
2 tsp melted coconut oil
1–2 tsp cinnamon, depending on taste
1 tsp pure vanilla extract

Directions

1. Preheat oven to 350°F.

2. Place oats on a baking sheet that has been lined with parchment paper and bake in oven for about 15 minutes, at which point oats should start to give off a nutty scent.

3. While oats are baking, combine honey, melted coconut oil, cinnamon and vanilla.

4. Once oats are done toasting, drizzle mixture over oats on baking sheet and stir to combine. Just be careful—the baking sheet will be hot.

5. Turn oven off and return sheet with oats to the oven. Let sit in the turned-off oven for 5–7 minutes.

6. Remove from oven and allow to cool. This can be eaten as is or used as a topping for yogurt, parfaits (pictured), ice cream and more.

If desired, ½–1 cup of nuts can be added to the oats prior to roasting.

Make sure to use parchment paper or a silicone baking mat, as the honey mixture can be sticky and hard to clean if placed directly on baking sheet.

I like to pack mine as a snack for studying with Twilight Sparkle!

127

Berry Baked Oatmeal

Makes 9 servings   **You can make this once and eat it all week!**

Ingredients

2	cups old-fashioned rolled oats
1½	tsp baking powder
½	tsp salt
1½	cups milk
¼	cup real maple syrup
1	large egg, beaten
2	tsp vanilla extract
2	cups mixed berries, washed, dried and cut

Directions

1. Preheat oven to 375°F. Spray a 2-quart baking pan with nonstick cooking spray. Set aside.

2. In a medium bowl, combine oats, baking powder and salt. Mix well to combine.

3. Add milk, syrup, egg and vanilla. Mix well to combine. Gently stir in berries.

4. Pour mixture into prepared baking pan and bake 20–25 minutes. Cool for 10 minutes prior to serving. If desired, serve in a bowl and top individual servings with milk.

It's so nice to start the day with a bowl full of berries!

Monkey Bread Muffins

Makes 12 muffins

These muffins are as fun to make as they are to eat!

Ingredients

1	can (about 16 oz) refrigerated biscuits
½	cup butter, melted
½	cup brown sugar
½	cup granulated sugar
3	tsp ground cinnamon
½	cup vanilla, buttercream or cream cheese frosting (opt)

Directions

1. Preheat oven to 350°F.

2. Mix melted butter with brown sugar and stir well. Set aside.

3. Mix granulated sugar and cinnamon in a large freezer-style zipper bag. Set aside.

4. Remove biscuits from can and cut each biscuit into eight pieces, as if you were slicing a pie. Once all pieces are cut, gently shape each piece into a more rounded shape.

5. Place all biscuit pieces into the bag with the cinnamon and sugar mixture and shake bag to coat each piece of biscuit with cinnamon and sugar.

6. Very generously coat a 12-count muffin pan with nonstick spray.

7. Stir melted butter and brown sugar mixture well, then place about 1 tablespoon of mixture into each cavity of the well-greased muffin pan.

8. Place 5–6 pieces of the cinnamon and sugar-covered biscuits into each cavity, on top of the butter and brown sugar mixture.

9. Place in the oven and bake for 13–15 minutes. Remove from oven and allow to cool for 1 minute. Then, immediately turn muffin pan upside down to remove muffins from pan. Muffins are served upside down. If desired, drizzle 2–3 teaspoons of frosting over the top of each muffin.

Messy pull-apart muffins are my favorite kind!

Cheesy Buttermilk Biscuits

Makes 6 biscuits **Double or triple this recipe—these biscuits go fast!**

Ingredients

- 1 cup cold buttermilk
- 8 Tbsp butter, divided
- 2 cups all-purpose flour, more for counter
- 1 Tbsp sugar
- ½ tsp baking soda
- 2 tsp baking powder
- ½ tsp garlic powder
- ½ tsp table salt
- 1 cup cheddar cheese, grated

I can't wait to share these with Cheese Sandwich!

Directions

1. Measure 1 cup of buttermilk and place in the freezer for 10 minutes

2. Place oven rack in middle position and preheat oven to 450°F. Line a baking sheet with parchment paper or a silicone baking mat, or spray a sheet pan with nonstick spray.

3. Place butter in a microwavable bowl, cover and heat for 30 seconds. If butter is not completely melted, return it to the microwave for 10-second intervals until melted. Set aside to cool.

4. Whisk together flour, sugar, baking soda, baking powder, garlic powder and salt in large bowl. Add grated cheese and mix together.

5. After buttermilk has been chilled in freezer for 10 minutes, combine it with the melted butter by pouring one into the other. Stir with a fork until the butter starts to form into small clumps in the buttermilk.

6. Add buttermilk mixture to dry ingredients and stir with rubber spatula just until all flour is incorporated and batter starts to pull away from sides of bowl.

Dough will be stiff and should not be overly sticky. If dough is too sticky, add more flour 1 tablespoon at a time, stirring to combine, until mixture has thickened.

7. Generously sprinkle flour over a countertop or work surface. Place biscuit dough onto prepared work surface and turn to coat all surfaces with flour.

8. Knead on counter 5–6 times. Flip over on work surface to coat with flour then pat into an approximately 6" square. It should be 1½–2" in height.

9. Cut biscuits with a 2½" round biscuit or cookie cutter. Place biscuits on prepared pan. Knead together any scraps until they hold together, then pat out to 1½–2" and cut additional biscuit(s). Transfer remaining biscuits to pan, spacing about 1½" apart.

10. Place in oven and bake until tops are golden brown and crisp. This can take anywhere from 8–15 minutes, so watch biscuits carefully to avoid burning. Remove from oven and enjoy.

Try topping them with melted butter and parsley!

Index

Recipe Index

Glossary

A

All-purpose flour
Flour that can be used for anything. If a recipe simply calls for "flour," use all-purpose flour.

B

Bake
To cook by surrounding with dry heat in an oven.

Batter
A pourable mixture of raw ingredients, like flour, eggs and oil.

Beat
To rapidly mix together ingredients, often with an electric mixer.

Blind-bake
To bake a pie crust or other pastry without the filling.

Broil
To cook by exposing to direct heat from above.

C

Combine
To mix together. To mix until "just combined," stop mixing as soon as you can't see the ingredient you just added.

Cream
To mix butter, usually with sugar, until it becomes lighter and more airy.

Crimp
To press together two pieces of dough, usually as a means to seal pie crust.

Crumb coat
A thin layer of frosting meant to trap any cake crumbs. Refrigerate a cake for 15 minutes after applying a crumb coat.

Curdle
A curdled mixture has separated from its mixed state. If eggs curdle in a cake batter, you can add a tablespoon of flour before mixing to recombine them.

Cut in
To add cold butter to a flour mixture using two knives, forks, a pastry blender or food processor. Once incorporated, the mixture will resemble coarse sand.

D

Dot
To evenly distribute small amounts of an ingredient (usually butter) over the top of a baked good.

Dough
A kneadable or scoopable mixture of raw ingredients.

Drizzle
To pour a narrow stream of liquid on top of something, often melted chocolate or a glaze.

Dust
To sprinkle lightly. You might dust a workspace with flour, or dust powdered sugar on top of baked goods.

E

Extract
A liquid with a concentrated flavor, like vanilla or almond.

F

Flute
To decoratively crimp the edges of a pastry, especially pie crust.

Fold
To gently combine ingredients, usually so as not to overmix or lose an airy texture.

G

Garnish
To decorate with something edible, like sprinkles.

Glaze
A thin topping, usually made of powdered sugar and milk or cream.

Grease

To liberally apply butter or oil so baked goods will not stick.

H

Heaping

A dry measurement that overflows the vessel, like a heaping tablespoon or cup. Do not level off "heaping" cups or spoons.

K

Knead

To mix dough using your hands, usually by folding it over, pressing down, turning and repeating.

L

Leavening agent

A substance that lightens and softens a dough or batter, helping it rise while baking. Baking soda, baking powder and yeast are all leavening agents.

O

Overmix

To mix a dough or batter more than necessary. Overmixing can make baked goods that are too chewy or dense.

P

Pipe

To apply frosting using a pastry bag.

Prepared

A prepared pan is one that has been greased or lined with a nonstick surface.

S

Score

To cut slits or lines into something. Pie crusts must be scored to let steam escape.

Sift

To put flour through a sifter, which adds air and breaks down any clumps.

Soft peaks

When whipping egg whites or cream, soft peaks are a stage where the "peaks" will bend or slump over.

Stiff peaks

When whipping egg whites or cream, stiff peaks are a stage where the "peaks" will stand straight up.

W

Whip

To beat quickly with a wire whisk or electric mixer. Whipping incorporates a lot of air into a mixture, making it lighter.

Y

Yield

The amount of servings a recipe will make.

Z

Zest

The finely grated skin of a citrus fruit, like lemon, lime or orange. When zesting a peel, stop when you see the white bitter part, known as the pith.

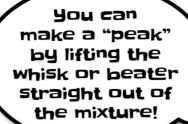

You can make a "peak" by lifting the whisk or beater straight out of the mixture!

Conversion Guide

Volume

¼ teaspoon = 1.25 mL

½ teaspoon = 2.5 mL

1 teaspoon = 5 mL

1 tablespoon = 15 mL

¼ cup = 60 mL

⅓ cup = 80 mL

½ cup = 120 mL

⅔ cup = 160 mL

¾ cup = 180 mL

1 cup = 240 mL

1 quart = 0.95 L

Weight

1 ounce = 28 grams

2 ounces = 57 grams

3 ounces = 85 grams

4 ounces (¼ pound) = 113 grams

8 ounces (½ pound) = 227 grams

16 ounces (1 pound) = 454 grams

2 pounds = 907 grams

Length

⅛ inch = 3 mm

¼ inch = 6 mm

½ inch = 13 mm

¾ inch = 19 mm

1 inch = 2½ cm

2 inches = 5 cm

Temperatures

32° Fahrenheit = 0° Celsius

212°F = 100°C	325°F = 160°C	425°F = 220°C
250°F = 120°C	350°F = 175°C	450°F = 230°C
275°F =135°C	375°F = 190°C	475°F = 245°C
300°F = 150°C	400°F = 205°C	500°F = 260°C

Birthday Cookie
Cake, p. 30

Baking is the best when you do it with friends!

Media Lab Books
For inquiries, call 646-838-6637

Copyright 2019 Topix Media Lab

Published by Topix Media Lab
14 Wall Street, Suite 4B
New York, NY 10005

Printed in China

ISBN-13: 978-1-948174-02-2
ISBN-10: 1-948174-02-2

Licensed by:

1C E19 1